NEW
Proficiency
Listening & Speaking

Fiona Scott-Barrett

Longman

EXAM FACTFILE

Paper 4: Listening	
takes	about 40 minutes.
is conducted in	groups.
consists of four parts:	**Part 1**: consists of four short extracts with two three-option multiple choice questions per extract. This tests ability to understand main ideas or details in a spoken text and/or to identify a speaker's feelings, attitudes, opinions, etc. **Part 2**: consists of nine sentence completion tasks based on a monologue. This tests ability to identify specific information. **Part 3**: consists of one long text with interacting speakers on which there are five four-option multiple choice questions. This tests ability to understand gist, details or opinions. **Part 4**: involves matching six statements about a discussion, debate or conversation to the speaker or speakers who made them. This tests ability to understand opinions, even if they are not stated directly, and to identify agreement or disagreement.
is marked	by giving one mark for each correct answer. Each candidate's raw score out of 28 is converted to a final score out of a total of 40 marks.

Paper 5: Speaking	
takes	about 19 minutes.
is conducted	by means of an interview. At the interview there will be an examiner who interacts with the candidates and asks questions (the interlocutor) and another (the assessor) who will not interact with the candidates but whose task is to assess the candidates' performance. The candidates will normally be interviewed in pairs.
consists of three parts:	**Part 1**: Some general, personal or social questions addressed to each candidate (about 3 minutes). **Part 2**: A collaborative task based on a picture or pictures (about 4 minutes). **Part 3**: Individual long turns based on prompt cards, followed by a discussion (about 12 minutes in total).
is assessed:	according to each candidate's performance in these areas: **grammatical resource**: Accuracy in using grammar and sentence structure **lexical resource**: appropriate and sufficiently wide use of vocabulary. **discourse management**: Ability to link ideas together appropriately. **pronunciation**: Acceptable and comprehensible pronunciation of individual sounds, words and complete sentences. **interactive communication**: Ability to take an active part in a discussion without hesitating too much. Each candidate is assessed on his/her own performance, not in relation to the other candidate. Marks are awarded out of a possible total of 40.

CONTENTS

Work and play

Listening A

Before you listen

Match the words (**1–6**) with the correct definitions (**a–f**).

1 an atrium

2 commute

3 a graduate

4 promotion prospects

5 a recruitment agency

6 tele-working

a a company which acts as an interface between companies who are looking for new employees and people who are looking for jobs

b a large high open space in a tall building

c opportunities for getting a more important job

d someone who has completed a university degree course

e the practice of working from home using telecommunications equipment to keep in touch with clients and colleagues

f travel a long distance to work every day

Part 1

In Part 1 of the Listening paper you will hear four short texts. These may be complete monologues or dialogues, or extracts from conversations or monologues. For each text there are two questions, each with three multiple choice options. You hear each extract twice before going on to the next one.

The questions may ask you to identify:
- *main ideas*
- *functions, e.g. apologising/ expressing regret*

- *the speaker's purpose (e.g. to persuade/inform/entertain the listener or other speaker)*
- *topics or feelings*
- *attitudes and opinions.*

Listening 1

a ▭ You will hear two different extracts. For questions **1–4**, choose the answer (**A**, **B** or **C**) which fits best according to what you hear.

Extract 1
You will hear a man talking on the radio about tele-working.

1 According to the speaker, what do people like about tele-working?

  A You work fewer hours.

  B You don't have to commute.

  C You have more time for friends and family.

     [1]

2 What does he feel about tele-workers', promotion prospects?

  A They may be overlooked when it comes to promotion.

  B Working from home has no effect on someone's promotion prospects.

  C Tele-working may improve someone's chances of being promoted.

     [2]

Extract 2
You will hear the owner of a recruitment agency talking about work.

3 What was the recruitment situation when the speaker left university?

  A Most graduates found jobs through recruitment agencies.

  B There were more graduates available than there were jobs.

  C Too many graduates had trained as engineers and lawyers.

     [3]

4 What is the speaker's view of young people nowadays compared to her generation?

  A They enjoy their jobs more.

  B Work is more important to them.

  C They are less concerned about how much they earn.

     [4]

b What words and phrases on the cassette helped you to identify the correct options? If necessary, listen to each extract a third time and identify the relevant words and phrases.

Part 2

In Part 2 you will hear one long monologue, such as a talk, lecture or broadcast. You have to complete nine gapped sentences which summarise the main ideas from the text. There is one gap per sentence which should be completed with one word or a short phrase from the text.

Listening 2

exam tip
In this task you write down the **exact words** you hear on the cassette. However, the words you need to write will not appear in the same context on the cassette and in the written sentences you have to complete.

a 🔊 You will hear a short extract from a monologue in which an architect is describing his plans for a new office building to the clients who commissioned him to design it. The words you hear on the tape and the sentence you have to complete are given below. Write the same words in the gap in the tapescript and the gap in the sentence for completion.

> **Tapescript**
> This then is the site plan. As you can see, the building is long and narrow and is aligned along a north–south axis, with a narrow side facing south. This means that it presents the smallest area to the ...., which helps to keep temperatures down in summertime.
>
> **Sentence**
> The end of the building which faces south is narrow so that the .... does not heat the building up too much.

b You will now hear the complete monologue. As you listen, complete sentences **1–7** below with a word or short phrase.

The clients asked for [1] in the building, therefore all the windows will open.

The building will feature [2] as well as those on the outside walls.

By opening all the windows, a [3] will be created to cool the working areas.

When the weather is very hot and humid, openings in the [4] will let out hot air.

The employees will work in [5] offices.

The shop will be located between the post room and the employees' [6] .

The [7] may be used for enjoying a drink or snack while having informal discussions with colleagues or visitors.

c Now listen again and check, complete or amend your answers.

Speaking A

Part 1

The Speaking paper is in the form of an interview which involves four people – two candidates, one examiner who asks questions and talks to the candidates, and another examiner who listens and assesses the candidates.

Part 1 of the interview takes about three minutes, during which the examiner takes turns to put different questions to each candidate. This part of the interview usually includes:

- *a question about where you live or with whom or about how you got to the interview.*
- *a more open question about your work or studies, your home or your interests.*
- *a question which requires you to speculate or offer an opinion in your answer.*

Personal questions `Interview, Part 1`

a Work with a partner. Read each question below and decide which answer (**A** or **B**) you think is less appropriate and why.

1 What kind of journey did you have to get here today?

  A I came by bus.

  B Rather a nerve-wracking one, I must say. My bus arrived twenty minutes late, so I was worried I wouldn't get here on time.

2 Are you studying or do you work? Could you tell us something about it?

  A Certainly. I've just started my first job, as a hotel receptionist. My job involves quite a lot of correspondence as well as face-to-face contact with our clients. We often have foreign guests in the hotel, so I get to use my English and German quite regularly.

  B I work for a small import–export company here. I like my job very much. I have been doing this job for two years and before that I was at business school.

3 What are employment opportunities like in this area?

  A They are very good, I think. Very few people don't have jobs in this area.

  B Somewhat limited, unfortunately. Most of the available jobs are seasonal because they're linked to tourism, so many young people move away in search of better opportunities.

4 How ambitious are you?

  A I would say I'm very ambitious. I want to be a surgeon when I grow up.

  B Not terribly. I hope to get a good job with a reasonable income, but my work would never be the most important thing in my life.

b How would *you* answer questions **1–4** above?

---

exam tip

The questions in this part of the interview are quite simple, to help you relax and warm up. Nevertheless, your answers in this part still contribute to your assessment.

Therefore:

- avoid very short answers. Try to include some details in your responses.
- link your ideas together with appropriate connectors (e.g. *so, though, as well*) and conversational words and phrases (e.g. *certainly, I would/must say, unfortunately, in general,* etc.)

Part 2

Part 2 of the Speaking paper lasts about four minutes. You will be shown one or more photographs and asked to comment on them, then to take part in a collaborative task with your partner.

Commenting on the photographs Interview, Part 2

Work with a partner. Look at photographs **1** and **2** and discuss where you think each photograph has been taken and what you think the people are doing.

Collaborative task Interview, Part 2

Work with a partner. Imagine that a large multinational company is preparing a brochure to use when recruiting new graduates. Discuss together and decide which of the photos (**1–5**) they should or should not include in the brochure in order to attract the best candidates, and why.

Useful words and phrases

high-tech equipment   state-of-the-art technology   a computer terminal   teamwork
a laptop computer   an open plan office   a workstation   (to) do overtime
work late   (to) do business internationally   video-based training seminar
(to) participate in a video-conference   cramped/overcrowded working conditions

I think this photo would/would not be suitable because it conveys an image of ...
Perhaps they should/should not include this picture because it gives the impression that ...
Yes, but on the other hand ...
I don't entirely agree. It seems to me that ...
OK, so we'll include/eliminate that photo, then.

Listening B

Before you listen

Mark the words and phrases below **D** if they are associated with danger or risk, **B** if they are associated with boredom or lack of interest, or **E** if they are associated with enthusiasm.

a jaded appetite	**blasé**	**crazy about**	**dice with death**	**mope around**
passionate about	**your heart in your mouth**		**scared out of your wits**	

Part 3

In Part 3 of the Listening paper you will hear one long text with interacting speakers, such as a broadcast interview or discussion. You have to answer five four-option multiple choice questions about the text which focus on a detailed understanding of the points raised in the interview or discussion.

Listening 1   Exam task, Part 3

a 〇〇 You will hear a radio programme on holidays. For questions **1–5**, choose the answer (**A**, **B**, **C** or **D**) which fits best according to what you hear.

1 Seaside holidays are
   A no longer fashionable.
   B available in exotic locations.
   C cheaper than ever before.
   D popular with people who like sleeping on beaches.

   [1]

2 The latest holiday trend is
   A to stay at home and learn something new.
   B to indulge in dangerous activities.
   C to go on activity holidays abroad.
   D to take several short breaks.

   [2]

3 Lake Geneva
   A appeals mainly to elderly holidaymakers.
   B is famous for its elegant hotels.
   C is not an obvious choice for an activity holiday.
   D is located in wild countryside.

   [3]

4 The reporter began to regret his decision to try canyoning because
   A he had to wear a wetsuit.
   B the sport wasn't challenging enough.
   C he was cold and frightened.
   D he forgot to hold onto the rope.

   [4]

5 At the end of the day the reporter
   A realised the sport was easier than he'd first thought.
   B felt miserable and uncomfortable.
   C was surprised to have survived the experience.
   D felt happy and excited.

   [5]

b Now listen again and check, complete or amend your answers.

Part 4

In Part 4 of the Listening paper you will hear one long conversation or informal discussion with two interacting speakers. Six statements summarise the main points raised in the conversation or discussion. You have to match each statement to the speaker who expresses that view, or to indicate where the speakers are in agreement.

Listening 2

exam tip	

You will not hear the same words on the cassette as appear in the statements. Therefore you need to:

- listen for opinions which express the emotions, attitudes or beliefs in the statements in different words.

- listen for expressions of agreement or disagreement (though you may not hear the actual words 'I agree' or 'I disagree') so that you are aware of each speaker's reactions to what the other one says.

a Read the instructions for the task, and statement 1 in **d** below.

b An extract from the tapescript of this conversation is reproduced here. First, underline the words in the tapescript which support statement 1. Then underline any words which express agreement or disagreement.

> Father: What on earth is the matter with Timothy? It's not healthy for a young lad like that to be moping around indoors all day.
>
> Sarah: I don't know what you're talking about, Dad. There's nothing the matter with him at all, and he's certainly not moping – he's got lots of interests.

c What would you write in answer to question 1 in **d** below?

d 📼 You will hear a man and his daughter, Sarah, having a conversation about her children, Timothy and Rebecca. For questions **1–6**, decide whether the opinions are expressed by only one of the speakers, or whether the speakers agree.

Write: (F) for the father, (S) for Sarah or (B) for both, where they agree.

1 Timothy appears to be bored or depressed. ☐
2 Young people should participate in sports. ☐
3 Rebecca is more physically active than Timothy. ☐
4 There is too much emphasis on competition in sports. ☐
5 Timothy's skill in using a computer is impressive. ☐
6 Sarah's father doesn't understand young people and their interests. ☐

e Listen again and check, complete or amend your answers.

f What words and phrases on the cassette helped you to find the correct answers to items **2–6**? If necessary, listen to the conversation a third time and identify the relevant words and phrases.

Speaking B

Commenting on the photographs Interview, Part 2

Work with a partner. Together compare and contrast the people and activities shown in photographs
1 and **2**.

Collaborative task Interview, Part 2

Work with a partner. Imagine that a photographic exhibition is being assembled on the theme of
Recreation. All these photographs are to be included. Talk together about the aspects of 'recreation'
the photographers are trying to show. Then suggest two other aspects of recreation which you
would like to see represented in the exhibition.

> **Useful words and phrases**
>
> active   amusing   artistic   competitive   contemplative
> creative   energetic   entertaining   informative   mental
> physical   relaxing   sociable   solitary   stimulating
>
> This photograph focuses on ... while the other shows ...
> I think the topic of 'recreation' encompasses ... as well as ...
> What is not illustrated/covered by any of these photos is/are ...

Part 3

Part 3 of the Speaking paper lasts about eleven minutes. It has the following steps:

- *Candidate A talks for about two minutes on a topic, based on a prompt card.*
- *The interviewer asks Candidate B a question about A's talk.*
- *The interviewer addresses one more question related to the topic of A's talk to both Candidates together.*
- *The steps above are repeated, with Candidate B talking and Candidate A listening.*
- *The examiner asks further questions related to both topics to open up a discussion between both Candidates.*

Long turn Interview, Part 3

Look at the prompt card below. In the long turn, you must talk about the question at the top of the card. The three points below the question are given as ideas to help you with appropriate content for your talk and as suggestions as to how you might organise it.

Prompt card

> In what ways have school-aged children's patterns of play changed in recent years?
>
> ▶ toys and activities
> ▶ leisure technology
> ▶ spending power

a Which points on the prompt card do the ideas (**a–d**) below relate to?

> **a** Children nowadays spend less time playing outdoors than previous generations did.
> **b** Most families in the western world are far more affluent than their parents' generation were.
> **c** Children seem to grow out of playing games together and to develop an interest in music or hand-held electronic games from quite an early age.
> **d** There are far more opportunities for entertainment in the home than before. As well as TV, many families now also have videos, computers or Internet access.

b Now match the ideas (**a–d**) to the reasons or results (**1–4**) below.

> **1** This means that they spend less time developing their skills of imagination and creative play.
> **2** One reason for this may be their parents' fears about their physical safety.
> **3** Children have therefore become much more sedentary than they used to be.
> **4** As a result, they are able to purchase greater quantities of toys, or to pay for their children to take part in out-of-school classes, hobbies or sporting activities.

c Think of one more idea for each of the points on the prompt card, along with a supporting reason or a result.

d Organise, then give a short talk on, the topic given in the prompt card. Include all the points from exercises **a** to **c** in this section. Use appropriate connectors to link your ideas together.

> **Useful words and phrases**
>
> as a result (of this)   this means that   consequently   therefore
> this is because   this is (probably) due to   in addition   what's more
> another factor/change/point is that

Man and the environment

Listening A

Think about the topic

1 How does man affect the environment?   **2** How does the environment affect man?

Before you listen

Write the words and phrases in the box in the correct part of the chart.

a drought	a flood	a shock wave	a tidal wave	a tremor
arid	casualties	humid	the death toll	

a lot of water	a lack of water	earthquakes	victims of natural disasters

Listening 1

a ◻◻ You will hear three different extracts. For questions **1–6**, choose the answer (**A**, **B** or **C**) which fits best according to what you hear.

Extract 1

You will hear two people discussing a newspaper article.

1 What do they disagree about?

   A Whether animals behave strangely before earthquakes or not.
   B The usefulness of the research being done in Kobe, Japan.
   C The importance of trying to predict earthquakes.

> 1

2 What is the woman's view of the usual scientific approach to earthquake prediction?
   A It is a waste of time and money.
   B It is the best method currently available.
   C It has its limitations.

> 2

Extract 2

You will hear a radio news bulletin about a natural disaster in Florida.

3 How many casualties have the tornadoes caused so far?
   A 36 or more.
   B About 200.
   C At least 236.

> 3

4 Why were the tornado warnings ineffective?
   A The authorities failed to emphasise how serious the situation was.
   B They were issued at the wrong time.
   C The danger only became apparent when most people were asleep.

> 4

Extract 3

You will hear a woman talking about a natural disaster and how it has affected her.

5 What kind of natural disaster is the woman describing?
   A A tidal wave.
   B An earthquake.
   C A flood.

> 5

6 Whom does the woman blame for the damage in her kitchen?
   A Herself.
   B The plumber.
   C No one.

> 6

b What words and phrases on the cassette helped you to identify the correct options?
If necessary, listen to each extract a third time and identify the relevant words and phrases.

Listening 2

a Look at sentences **1–6** in **c** below. Choose which group of words (**a–f**) might fill the gaps in these sentences.

a high / low	**d** wind / current / breeze
b higher / lower	**e** direction / force / strength
c dry / wet / arid / humid	**f** water / sea / ocean

b Work with a partner and try to anticipate what words might fill the gaps in sentences **7–9** in **c** below.

c ◼◻ You will hear a lecture about a climatic phenomenon called El Niño. For questions **1–9**, complete the sentences with a word or short phrase.

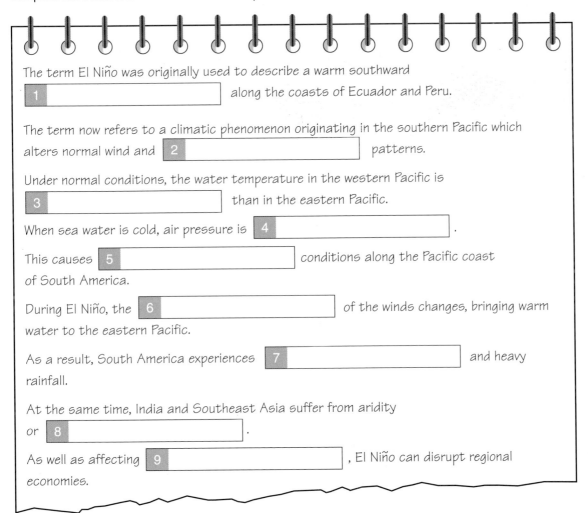

The term El Niño was originally used to describe a warm southward

[1 _____] along the coasts of Ecuador and Peru.

The term now refers to a climatic phenomenon originating in the southern Pacific which alters normal wind and [2 _____] patterns.

Under normal conditions, the water temperature in the western Pacific is

[3 _____] than in the eastern Pacific.

When sea water is cold, air pressure is [4 _____].

This causes [5 _____] conditions along the Pacific coast of South America.

During El Niño, the [6 _____] of the winds changes, bringing warm water to the eastern Pacific.

As a result, South America experiences [7 _____] and heavy rainfall.

At the same time, India and Southeast Asia suffer from aridity or [8 _____].

As well as affecting [9 _____], El Niño can disrupt regional economies.

d Now listen again and check, complete or amend your answers.

Speaking A

Commenting on the photographs Interview, Part 2

Work with a partner. Look at photographs **2** and **4** and discuss what you think might have led up to the situations you see in the photographs.

Collaborative task Interview, Part 2

Work with a partner. Imagine that a charity is planning a newspaper advertising campaign to raise money to help the victims of natural disasters worldwide. Discuss together and decide which, if any, of these photographs should appear in the advertisement. If you think none of these photographs would be particularly effective in encouraging people to make donations, suggest alternative images which would work better.

Useful words and phrases

heaps of rubble   shattered chunks of concrete   (to) collapse
a wall of fire   (to) go up in flames   an act of arson
(to) get out of control   (to) identify with (someone)
(to) elicit (someone's) sympathy   (to) portray the despair/
helplessness/shock felt by …

Shall we discuss each photo in turn?

My feeling is that this picture focuses more on … than …

It seems to me that this image conjures up …

What do you think about this one? / What's your view?

Yes, I hadn't thought of that. / That's a good point.

I see your point, but …

What might be more effective, then? / What would put that idea/message over more forcefully?

exam tip

Remember that the purpose of this task is to show your ability to interact in a discussion with another person. Therefore:

- take turns to speak.
- ask your partner for his/her comments, ideas and reactions, as well as stating your own opinions.
- listen to what your partner says and react to his/her ideas and suggestions.

Long turn Interview, Part 3

a Look at prompt cards **a** and **b** below and the list of phrases. Decide which prompt card each phrase goes with.

Prompt card a

What problems do natural disasters cause?
▸ the victims themselves
▸ local infrastructure
▸ national economy

Prompt card b

How might the effects of earthquakes be reduced?
▸ prediction
▸ building methods
▸ rescue work

a	animal behaviour	**j**	monitoring tremors and geological changes
b	banning construction on soft ground / in high-risk areas	**k**	payment of compensation / insurance claims
c	cost of rebuilding	**l**	provision of adequate equipment and funding for emergency services
d	death or injury		
e	disruption of usual economic activities	**m**	psychological problems, e.g. shock, fear, anxiety
f	earthquake-resistant materials and methods	**n**	recruiting and training volunteers to be on stand-by in an emergency
g	interruption of essential services, e.g. gas, water, electricity, transport	**o**	stricter legislation on construction methods
h	loss of/damage to property	**p**	training for rescue teams in responding rapidly to a crisis
i	loss of income		

b Work in pairs. Student A prepares a short talk based on prompt card **a**. Student B prepares a short talk based on prompt card **b**. Use appropriate phrases from the list in **a** above, and organise your points, following the prompts on the card. You may include other ideas of your own if you want to.

c **Student A** gives his/her talk. Student B listens. At the end of the talk, B answers this question: *Is there anything you would like to add to what student A said?*

d **Student B** gives his/her talk. Student A listens. At the end of the talk, A answers this question: *Is there anything student B said that you don't agree with?*

Listening B

Before you listen

Complete the table, using the words and phrases in the box.

| car exhaust fumes | oil spills | water pollution | rise in earth's temperature |
| increased risk of skin cancer | untreated sewage | breathing problems, e.g. asthma | soil erosion |

Causes ➡	Environmental problems ➡	Long-term effects
• deforestation	1 .... • build-up of carbon dioxide in atmosphere	• loss of plant and animal species 2 ....
3 .... • factory emissions • burning fossil fuels	• air pollution	4 .... • rise in earth's temperature
5 .... 6 .... • overuse of chemicals in agriculture	7	• loss of marine species • destruction of coral reefs
• use of aerosols and coolants that contain CFCs	• depletion of the ozone layer	8 .... • rise in earth's temperature

Listening 1

> **exam tip**
>
> Sometimes two or more options in multiple choice questions may at first seem to be correct. As you are listening the first time, mark all possible options with a tick or a question mark. When you hear the tape the second time, listen specifically for things said on the tape which either support or contradict the options you have already marked as being possible answers.

a 🔊 You will hear a radio interview with Maggie Kerr, who launched the 'Down with Noise' campaign. For questions **1–4**, choose the alternative (**A**, **B**, **C** or **D**) which fits best according to what you hear.

1 According to Maggie Kerr, high levels of noise
  A have been reduced in towns and cities.
  B are recognised as a problem by the World Health Organisation.
  C are recognised as a health risk by most members of the public.
  D can cause asthma in children.

  [1]

2 Maggie Kerr
  A had a history of blood pressure problems.
  B went to her doctor for advice on how to handle stress.
  C was lucky that her doctor believed her.
  D became ill as a result of a change in her immediate environment.

  [2]

3 Noise constitutes a health hazard
  A mainly for people who suffer from stress.
  B mainly for people who live near airports.
  C when people are exposed to above-average noise levels over a long period.
  D when people are exposed to very high noise levels for short periods.

[3]

4 The 'Down with Noise' campaign
  A wants to reduce bus traffic in towns.
  B shares some of the aims of other environmental groups.
  C organises national campaigns against cars.
  D works together with Environmental Health Officers.

[4]

b After listening to the tape the first time, compare the options you have marked as possible with a partner. Have you chosen the same ones?

c Now listen again and check, complete or amend your answers.

d What words and phrases on the cassette helped you to identify the correct options? If necessary, listen a third time and identify the relevant words and phrases.

Listening 2 Exam task, Part 4

exam tip

In Part 4 tasks, opinions may be phrased as questions, or implied rather than stated directly.

a An extract from the start of a radio interview about coral reefs is reproduced below. What is the interviewer implying?
  1 Divers are the main cause of the destruction to coral reefs.
  2 Taking tourists diving may endanger coral reefs.

Interviewer: Paul, your company specialises in diving holidays, and the report states that nearly 60% of the world's coral reefs are at risk from human activity. How does that make you feel about the business you're involved in?

Paul Wrightsman: Well, if you're trying to make me feel guilty, I'd like to point out that we have always aimed to be an environmentally sensitive organisation. Everyone who travels with us gets a lecture at the start of their holiday about showing respect for the environment they're visiting. For example, we tell them it's totally unacceptable to chip bits off coral reefs to take home as souvenirs or to hunt rare fish species.

b ▣ You will hear two people, Paul and Judy, discussing an environmental report about coral reefs. For questions **1–6** decide whether the opinions are expressed by only one of the speakers, or whether the speakers agree.

Write: Ⓟ for Paul, Ⓙ for Judy or Ⓑ for both, where they agree.

1 Irresponsible tourists might deliberately damage coral reefs. ☐
2 Tourism inevitably has a negative environmental impact. ☐
3 Sewage discharge destroys coral reefs and marine species. ☐
4 The coral reefs at greatest risk are in poor regions of the world. ☐
5 Agricultural methods can contribute to water pollution. ☐
6 Legislation regarding fishing methods ought to be tighter. ☐

c Now listen again and check, complete or amend your answers.

d Listen a third time, and note the ways in which the speakers expressed their opinions.

Speaking B

Commenting on the photographs Interview, Part 2

Work with a partner. Look at photograph **2** and talk together about what you think the photographer's purpose was in taking this photograph.

Collaborative task Interview, Part 2

Work with a partner. Imagine that an environmental organisation is preparing a leaflet to be distributed to the public. Their aim is to raise people's awareness of how their own habits can affect the environment. All the photos are to appear in the leaflet. Discuss what aspect of people's behaviour each photograph is illustrating, and what individuals can do differently in order to reduce their impact on the environment.

> **Useful words and phrases**
>
> bumper-to-bumper traffic   congestion   an open dump   piles of rubbish
> bleaches/detergents/cleaning products   toxic   reliance on   over-enthusiastic use of
> over-consumption of   disregard for the long-term consequences of   (to) consume
> (to) discard   (to) re-use   (to) recycle   eco-friendly products   car-pooling
>
> The photographs shows … so I think the point he/she is trying to make is …
> I think the photographer's aim is to …
> This picture illustrates the way in which we … and thus …
> This clearly shows how our … leads to/results in …
> People should/ought to … instead of …
> … would/might not be so severe/widespread if we …

Long turn Interview, Part 3

a Work in two groups to prepare a short talk.

Group A
Look at prompt card **a**. Use the chart in Before you listen in Listening B (page 16) to help you with ideas and vocabulary.

Group B
Look at prompt card **b**. Use the chart in Before you listen in Listening B (page 16) to help you with ideas and vocabulary.

Prompt card a

What changes have taken place in the environment as a result of man's activities?

▶ air
▶ water
▶ climate

Prompt card b

What measures can governments take to reduce pollution?

▶ transport systems
▶ power generation
▶ legislation

b Now form pairs of one **A** and one **B**. Follow the steps below:

- A gives his/her talk. B listens.
- The teacher asks B a question about A's talk.
- B answers the question about A's talk.
- Exchange roles until each of you has had a chance to give your talk and answer a question.

exam tip

Remember to listen carefully to your partner's talk so that you can refer to what he/she said when you answer the question.

Follow-up questions Interview, Part 3

Now discuss these questions with a partner.

- Do you care about the environment?
- To what extent can changes an individual makes in his/her lifestyle really help to protect the environment?
- What do you think is the single biggest environmental threat we face today?

Relationships

Listening A

Think about the topic

1 How important are family relationships to you?

2 In what way have relationships within families changed since your parents were young?

3 What role, if any, do animals play in your life?

Before you listen

Explain the differences between the words in each group.

1	2	3
• an extended family • a nuclear family • a single-parent family	• a childminder • a babysitter • a nursery school	• to keep someone company • to be/not be good company • to keep company with (a group of people)

Listening 1

🔲 You will hear two different extracts. For questions **1–4**, choose the answer (**A**, **B** or **C**) which fits best according to what you hear.

Extract 1

You will hear the start of a radio interview with a couple who have an unusual relationship.

1 The man's job used to involve

  A information technology.
  B administration.
  C property management.

          1

2 He thinks the term 'househusband' is
  A offensive.
  B inaccurate.
  C appropriate.

          2

Extract 2

You will hear two friends talking about teenagers.

3 What do they disagree about?

  A The extent to which teenagers have changed.
  B The need for young people to show their independence.
  C The methods by which teenagers reject their parents' ideas.

          3

4 What does the woman feel about communication problems between teenagers and their parents?

  A They are the parents' fault.
  B They can usually be avoided.
  C They exist only in some families.

          4

Listening 2 `Exam task, Part 4`

a ▱ The radio interview you heard in Listening1, Extract 1 continues. You will hear Alec and Penny discussing their relationship. For questions **1–6**, decide whether the opinions are expressed by only one of the speakers, or whether the speakers agree.

Write: (A) for Alec, (P) for Penny or (B) for both, where they agree.

1 Their way of life evolved out of their different attitudes to the importance of work. ☐
2 Their domestic arrangement suits the family well. ☐
3 Hired domestic helpers are never one hundred per cent trustworthy. ☐
4 No ill feeling exists between the couple over financial arrangements. ☐
5 Other people's reactions to Alec and Penny's situation can be irritating. ☐
6 Alec works hard at his domestic duties. ☐

b Now listen again and check, complete or amend your answers.

Listening 3 `Exam task, Part 3`

a ▱ You will hear an interview with Kathy, a British woman who lives in Greece and is married to a Greek man. She is talking about the differences between family life in Britain and Greece. For questions **1–5**, choose the answer (**A**, **B**, **C** or **D**) which fits best according to what you hear.

1 In comparing British and Greek families, Kathy thinks that
   A the British have fewer children.
   B more British couples get divorced than Greek ones.
   C Greek families are more affected by employment patterns.
   D Greek families are closer-knit.

☐ 1

2 Being surrounded by family members
   A was the usual condition of Kathy's childhood.
   B was a rare experience for Kathy before her marriage.
   C makes Kathy feel she needs more space.
   D has appealed to Kathy since her son was born.

☐ 2

3 Kathy gets frustrated in Greece because
   A she feels lonely.
   B she is not allowed to make her own decisions.
   C family members are constantly asking her for help.
   D family members are constantly giving her advice.

☐ 3

4 As a working mother, Kathy
   A has had to change her schedule every week.
   B has had to find a childminder.
   C finds life easier in Greece than Britain.
   D is forced to rely on the family for help.

☐ 4

5 Kathy thinks Dimitris' brother's mother-in-law
   A is being used by her family.
   B is too ill to be expected to cook.
   C enjoys her household duties.
   D would be better off in a nursing home.

☐ 5

b Now listen again and check, complete or amend your answers.

Speaking A

Commenting on the photographs Interview, Part 2

Work with a partner. Look at photographs **1** and **2** and compare and contrast the people and situations shown.

Collaborative task Interview, Part 2

Work with a partner. Imagine that a magazine is publishing a feature entitled 'The Family Today' and is considering using some of these photographs to accompany the article. Talk together about what aspect of family life each photograph depicts, then decide which photographs would be appropriate to include with an article on family life in the country you live in.

Useful words and phrases

a family gathering   a celebration   (to) propose a toast
(to) feed   a highchair   a boardgame   a laundry basket   a dispute
a conflict   (to) wrangle   convivial   intimate   harassed
overwrought   embarrassed   distressed/disturbed   (to) bond with
(to) withdraw (from)   (to) be torn between two parents/sides

Discussion Interview, Part 3

a Read the two questions for discussion below and the notes given below each question. Mark each note with a tick (✓) if it supports the idea in the question, or a cross (✗) if it is an argument against the idea in the question.

1 Should women with young children go out to work?

    a finding suitable childcare options can be problematic

    b benefits of a second income

    c difficulties when children are ill

    d stress due to pressures of balancing work and household duties

    e stimulation provided by contacts outside the home

2 Do grandparents still have a role to play in families?

    a help with childcare and domestic chores

    b sometimes out of touch with modern habits and lifestyles

    c experience of life and common problems

    d knowledge about the family's history

    e may have old-fashioned ideas about discipline and child-rearing

b Think of one or two more ideas of your own for each question.

c Work with a partner. Discuss the two questions in **a** above.

Useful phrases

I think it depends very much on ...
On the whole, I think they should/shouldn't/do/don't as ...
Based on my own experience I would say that ...
On the other hand, this advantage/disadvantage may be outweighed by ...
I take your point about ..., but I think you also have to consider ...
That's true in some cases, but you also have to take ... into account.

Listening B

Before you listen

a Explain the differences between the words and phrases in each group.

1 • natural habitat   • in the wild   • in captivity

2 • a poacher   • a hunter   • a predator

b Complete the gaps in the short text about cloning below with the words and phrases in the box.

| adult cell | embryo | host mother | nucleus |

First the **1** .... is removed from an egg cell; then it is replaced with the nucleus from an **2** ...., and thirdly the resulting **3** .... is implanted in a **4** ....

Listening 1 Exam task, Part 2

a Look at questions **1–9** in **b**. What kind of word or information will you be listening for to answer each question? Choose from the following possibilities and write the number of the corresponding question (**1–9**) in the correct box.

a an adjective ☐
b an animal or animals ☐
c a chemical product or products ☐
d a condition or medical problem (x 2) ☐

e a country or countries ☐
f a noun relating to people or parts of people ☐
g a noun used when comparing or contrasting ☐
h a number ☐

b 🔊 You will hear a short lecture about animal testing. For questions **1–9**, complete the sentences with a word or short phrase.

About **1** [____] animals die in Britain each year during or after animal experiments.

The LD50 test involved administering increasing doses of a chemical until half the **2** [____] being tested died.

The authorities in **3** [____] initially opposed the abolition of the LD50 test.

It is not **4** [____] for any pharmaceutical company to license a new product unless it has been tested on animals.

In Britain, animal testing of **5** [____] is not permitted.

In the 1960s children were born with **6** [____] caused by a drug which had passed all the necessary animal tests.

In 1997 a substantial number of people suffered **7** [____] as a result of taking a drug which had had no ill effects on animals.

The speaker considers that animal testing provides inaccurate information where humans are concerned because there are insufficient **8** [____] between the species.

Computers can now be used to simulate the effects of drugs on human **9** [____].

c Now listen again and check, complete or amend your answers.

Listening 2 Exam task, Part 3

a 🔊 You will hear a radio programme about the giant panda. For questions **1–5**, choose the answer (**A**, **B**, **C** or **D**) which fits best according to what you hear.

1 Why does Pauline O'Grady say pandas are 'ill-equipped for survival'?

  A Their natural habitat is being destroyed.

  B They eat too much.

  C Male pandas greatly outnumber female ones.

  D A large number of pandas are unable to reproduce.

  `1`

2 Panda cubs frequently do not survive because

  A they are very small at birth.

  B the mother is unable to feed them.

  C they are killed unintentionally by an adult panda.

  D the mother refuses to look after them.

  `2`

3 The biggest threat to pandas in the wild is

  A their source of food has been depleted.

  B they are hunted for their skins.

  C they are captured for zoos.

  D they are defenceless against predators.

  `3`

4 The main difference between cloning sheep and cloning pandas would be

  A the steps of the process would be performed in a different order.

  B more species would be involved.

  C the process would take longer.

  D more attempts would need to be made for the process to succeed.

  `4`

5 According to Pauline O'Grady, the Chinese plan to clone pandas because

  A breeding programmes in zoos have not been successful.

  B success in doing so would generate respect internationally.

  C they like finding technical solutions to complex problems.

  D they are unwilling to spend money on restoring the panda's natural habitat.

  `5`

b Now listen again and check, complete or amend your answers.

Speaking B

Commenting on the photographs   Interview, Part 2

Work with a partner. Look at photograph **3** and discuss together what emotions this image evokes in you.

Collaborative task   Interview, Part 2

Work with a partner. Imagine that an animal rights group is compiling an album of photos showing man's cruelty to animals. The album will be shown to passers-by in the streets with the intention of encouraging members of the public to donate money to their cause. Discuss together and decide which of these photographs it would be appropriate to include in the album, and why, and whether there are any other images which you think should be included.

Useful words and phrases

primitive tribe/hunter   cheetah/leopard   animal hide/skin   customs   way of life   (to) humiliate
heavy load/burden   firewood   ill-treatment   rural community   untouched by the passage of time
bull fighting   matador   cape   blood sports   cruelty to animals   (to) take pleasure in …
(to) put up a good fight   the odds are stacked against someone   (to) goad the bull   factory farming
artificial lighting   cramped conditions   packed   (to) make an animal look ridiculous

Perhaps photograph … may not be appropriate because …
I don't think that … could really be considered as cruel …
You have to admit that there is a difference between … and …
… hardly qualifies as cruelty to animals.
The picture which I think people will find most shocking/disgusting is …

Long turn Interview, Part 3

a Work in pairs. Student A prepares a short talk based on prompt card a. Student B prepares a short talk based on prompt card **b**.

Prompt card a

> How have man's relationships with animals changed across the years?
>
> ▶ hunter-gatherer societies
> ▶ agricultural communities
> ▶ urban, technologically advanced societies

Note: The photos on page 26 should help you with ideas. Add any ideas and examples of your own too.

Prompt card b

> How are attitudes to the use of animals changing nowadays?
>
> ▶ farming methods
> ▶ sport and entertainment
> ▶ testing of health and beauty products

Note: Photographs 3, 4 and 5 and your notes on Listening B1 should help you with ideas. Add any ideas and examples of your own too.

Useful words and phrases

the hunter and the hunted   a source of food/clothing/income
beasts of burden   a means of transport   a sentimental attachment (to)
organic farming   cruelty-free products   repellent/distasteful/disturbing

In such societies the relationship is primarily one of ... / animals are regarded mainly as ...
It is mainly in ... societies/communities that ...
Nowadays, more and more people are turning to/against ...
I think that people find ... increasingly ...

b **Student A** gives his/her talk. Student B listens. At the end of the talk, B answers this question. *What do you think?*

c **Student B** gives his/her talk. Student A listens. At the end of the talk, A answers this question. *How does this differ from your experience?*

Follow-up questions Interview, Part 3

Now work with a different partner and discuss these questions.

> • What can children learn from keeping pets?
> • Should all types of hunting be banned?
> • Do you agree with the saying. 'A dog is a man's best friend.'
> • Do zoos do more harm than good?

Young people in society

Listening A

Think about the topic

1 How important is a good education in young people's lives?
2 What problems and difficulties do young people face nowadays?

Before you listen

Write the words and phrases in the box in the correct part of the chart.

> A-levels   articulate   co-educational classes / schools   coherent
> creativity   degree   intellect   junior / senior high school (US)   knowledge
> literacy   primary school (UK)   secondary school (UK)
> segregated classes / schools   single sex classes / schools   university

Attributes of educated people		Educational establishments	Educational options	Qualifications
nouns	adjectives			

Listening 1

🔊 You will hear two different extracts. For questions **1–4**, choose the answer (**A**, **B** or **C**) which fits best according to what you hear.

Extract 1

You will hear a man and woman discussing the reintroduction of school uniforms at her daughter's school.

1 What did the man not like about his own school uniform?

   A It was uncomfortable.
   B It looked ridiculous.
   C It was too formal.

> 1

2 The woman is in favour of school uniforms because
   A they are casual and comfortable nowadays.
   B they benefit children from poor families.
   C most mothers dress their children inappropriately for school.

> 2

Extract 2

You will hear part of a radio broadcast about gifted children.

3 The speaker says the difference between gifted and talented children is that the latter

   A have had government help.
   B only have one field of excellence.
   C are easier to recognise as being different from other children.

> 3

4 Some gifted children do not get extra help or tuition because

   A it is too expensive.
   B adults fear this may harm them psychologically.
   C they are too immature to handle this.

> 4

Listening 2 Exam task, Part 2

a ◨◨ You will hear a radio programme about education. For questions **1–9**, complete the sentences with a word or short phrase.

Evidence of changes associated with puberty can be deeply [1 _____] for children in mixed sex classes.

Most British schools have opted for [2 _____] since the 1970s.

In recent years, it is [3 _____] who have performed better in exams.

Boys in their early teens are less [4 _____] than girls of the same age.

Boys give up trying to do well at school if they [5 _____] at an early stage of their teens.

Instead, they pretend to have little interest in [6 _____] and fool around in class.

Boys are usually much less [7 _____] than girls about making mistakes or annoying their teacher.

A lot of people believe that the idea of having [8 _____] is old-fashioned and unrealistic.

Nevertheless, it is possible that both sexes will perform better [9 _____] by having some, or all, of their classes separately.

b Now listen again and check, complete or amend your answers.

Listening 3 Exam task, Part 3

a ◨◨ You will hear a radio debate about education. For questions **1–5**, choose the answer (**A**, **B**, **C** or **D**) which fits best according to what you hear.

1 According to Anne, the main problem with the education system in Britain is
  A no one agrees about the curriculum that should be taught.
  B there is no discipline in schools.
  C no one believes in good manners anymore.
  D no one agrees about what its purpose should be. [1]

2 Anne says that the old concept of a well-educated person
  A encompassed personal qualities as well as knowledge.
  B deserved to be changed because it was elitist. [2]
  C has been replaced by a better concept.
  D led to people becoming over-educated.

3 Quentin believes that the education system
  A pleases examiners.
  B tests intellect and knowledge.
  C prepares young people for the challenges of the future. [3]
  D stunts creativity and original thinking.

4 Phil believes that
  A literacy is more important than creativity.
  B creativity is more important than literacy.
  C being well-educated encompasses creativity, originality and literacy. [4]
  D many creative people are unable to express themselves articulately.

5 What does Phil say about universities?
  A They focus too much on gaining qualifications.
  B They are not strict enough with their students.
  C They are easier to get into than they used to be. [5]
  D They produce more graduates than two decades ago.

b Now listen again and check, complete or amend your answers.

Speaking A

Personal questions Interview, Part 1

Work in pairs. Take turns to interview each other. When you are the interviewer, ask your partner one question from each group (**A–C**). When you are answering, remember the tips given in unit one, on page 6.

A Are you at school or university, or do you work?
Do you live near the place where you study English?

B Where did you go to primary school? Did you like it?
What are the main reasons that you are learning English?
What are your plans for the future?

C What skills do you think it will be important to learn in the future?
If you could change one thing about your past, what would it be?
What do you think are the most important life decisions you will have to make in the near future?

exam tip

Before you go for the interview make sure you know the correct vocabulary to:
- describe what you do now
- describe your future career path and/or plans for further education.

However, do not prepare speeches on these topics to learn by heart! The examiner will realise this and you will lose marks accordingly.

Commenting on the photographs Interview, Part 2

Work with a partner. Discuss what you think might have happened just before the photograph was taken.

Collaborative task Interview, Part 2

Work with a partner. Imagine that a private language school is preparing a new publicity brochure for the next academic year. They are considering using the photograph opposite on the front of the brochure. Discuss together what image of the school you think this picture would project and whether you think it would be likely to attract new students to the school. If you think it would not be successful as a publicity photo, talk about what alternative images might be more appropriate.

> **Useful words and phrases**
>
> formal/informal   traditional/innovative   strict/lax discipline
> teacher-led/activity-centred   collaborative   participative   rote learning
> learning by doing
>
> This might/might not appeal to students/their parents because ...
> This picture seems to me to create a .... image of the school.
> I would have thought that ...... might be more appropriate.
> Yes, but don't you think that might give the impression that ... ?

Long turn and follow-up Interview, Part 3

a Work in pairs. Student A prepares a short talk based on prompt card **a**. Student B prepares a short talk based on prompt card **b**.

Prompt card a

> To what extent are teachers responsible for their pupils' success in learning?
> ▶ motivation
> ▶ learners' natural ability
> ▶ curriculum

Prompt card b

> In what ways has education changed since you started school?
> ▶ aims
> ▶ curriculum
> ▶ teaching methods and activities

b **Student A** gives his/her talk. Student B listens. At the end of the talk, B answers this question:
Is there anything you don't agree with?

c **Student B** gives his/her talk. Student A listens. At the end of the talk, A answers this question:
How does this differ from your experience?

d Now discuss these questions with a different partner.

> - What should the aims of education be?
> - Should schoolchildren wear uniforms?
> - What qualities are important in a teacher?
> - Are exams the best way of testing a student's knowledge and intellect?

Listening B

Before you listen

Match the words (**1–6** and **a–e**) to make common word combinations. Two items in the column on the left can go with one of the words **a–e**. Use a dictionary to check the meanings if necessary.

1	illicit	**a**	model
2	general	**b**	group
3	local	**c**	election
4	peer	**d**	drugs
5	role	**e**	abuse
6	substance		

Listening 1

▭▭ You will hear two different extracts. For questions **1–4**, choose the answer (**A**, **B** or **C**) which fits best according to what you hear.

Extract 1

You will hear a young woman reminiscing about her schooldays.

1 What problem did the speaker suffer from at primary school?

   A She was unpopular because she was fat.
   B She couldn't keep up academically with the other pupils.
   C She was bullied by a classmate.

                                                                                     1

2 How did the speaker feel when the person she describes first disappeared?

   A Thankful.
   B Guilty.
   C Surprised.

                                                                                      2

Extract 2

You will hear a man and woman discussing their teenage son.

3 The man is upset because his son

   A wants to get married.
   B wants to give up his education.
   C wants to take a temporary job.

                                                                                      3

4 How does the woman feel about her husband's reaction?

   A Exasperated.
   B Sympathetic.
   C Disappointed.

                                                                                      4

Listening 2 Exam task, Part 2

a ▭▭ You will hear part of a lecture about substance abuse among high school students in the U.S. During the lecture the speaker uses the term ATOD to refer collectively to alcohol, tobacco and other drugs. For questions **1–9**, complete the sentences with a word or short phrase.

exam tip
In sentence completion tasks, you will lose marks in the exam if the words are not correctly spelt. This includes using capital letters where necessary.

A far higher percentage of American high school students have tried

| 1 | than have sampled illicit drugs.

American schools have been using education programmes to combat substance abuse for

| 2 | .

It is a common | 3 | among teenagers that everyone in their age group uses ATOD.

Many young people find it more difficult to talk to parents and teachers once they reach

| 4 | .

| 5 | , such as film stars or pop stars, may encourage teenagers to try ATOD.

Teenagers are less likely to try a drug if they believe it could cause them long-term

| 6 | .

Explanations of the consequences of ATOD are not | 7 | if they are too dramatic and frightening.

Another factor that discourages ATOD use is the development of high

| 8 | .

Some teenagers worry about | 9 | if they refuse to drink, smoke or take drugs.

b Now listen again and check, complete or amend your answers.

Listening 3 Exam task, Part 4

a ▭ You will hear a discussion between two teenagers, Cheryl and Richard. For questions **1–6**, decide whether the opinions are expressed by only one of the speakers, or whether the speakers agree.

Write: C for Cheryl, R for Richard or B for both, where they agree.

* Westminster is the seat of the British parliament.

1 National politics are boring. ☐
2 Economic policy affects minors. ☐
3 Politicians treat minors cynically. ☐
4 The current legislation concerning minors is illogical. ☐
5 Sixteen and seventeen year olds feel traditional politics are irrelevant to their lives. ☐
6 There's power in numbers. ☐

b Now listen again and check, complete or amend your answers.

Speaking B

Commenting on the photographs Interview, Part 2

Work with a partner. Look at photograph **1** and discuss how the boy seems to be feeling and why he might be in this situation.

Collaborative task Interview, Part 2

Work with a partner. Imagine that an international children's rights organisation is preparing its annual report. All these photographs are to be included. Discuss together and decide what issues they illustrate and what the organisation might have done to redress them.

Useful words and phrases

(to) campaign for/against   (to) alleviate poverty/suffering   (to) join the army
(to) eliminate the causes of   (to) raise/distribute funds (for/to)   child warrior
minor   guerilla warfare   civil war   fighter   machine gun   child poverty
(to) recruit/be recruited   revolutionary/freedom   loss of innocence
beggar   street children   homelessness   child labour   exploitation   fair trade
(to) campaign against   medical aid   voting rights   booth   secret ballot
ballot paper   democracy

Discussion Interview, Part 3

a Read the model below. It is an extract from a discussion about bullying at school.

> **A:** I think it's very important that a child in this situation should not keep silent about what's going on, but should go and see an authority.
>
> **B:** So you think they should go to the police, or an expert on this sort of problem, something like that?
>
> **A:** No, I mean to an adult, like a teacher at the school whom they trust, or maybe an uncle or aunt, if they're too embarrassed to discuss it with their parents, for example.
>
> **B:** I see. Yes, I think that's a good idea. Or alternatively …

*uses incorrect
vocabulary so her
idea is not clear*

*reformulates her
idea in different
words*

b What vocabulary mistake did A make that caused B to misunderstand?
How did B deal with A's error?

c Work with a partner. Discuss the questions below, following this plan.

A expresses an idea/opinion.
↓
B checks he/she has understood.
↓
A confirms B is right, or corrects him/her and reformulates the idea.
↓
B reacts and adds a further supporting idea/example or a contrasting idea/example.
↓
A checks he/she has understood.
↓
B confirms A is right, or corrects him/her and reformulates the idea.
↓
A reacts.

- Should the voting age be reduced?
- To what extent do peer group attitudes influence teenagers?
- What are the greatest threats to young people's happiness?
- How important are political issues to young people in your country?

Useful phrases
So, if I've understood correctly, you think/feel/believe that …
Sorry, but do you mean that … (or) …?
So, for example, … Is that what you mean?
Not exactly. What I mean/meant is/was …
No. Let me put it another way.
Not really. To put it in other words, …

Health and medicine

Listening A

Think about the topic

1 What illnesses are most prevalent in your country, and what do you think causes them?
2 What advances in modern medical science interest or impress you most?

Before you listen

Match the words (1–7) with the correct definitions (a–g).

1	to consult	a	a doctor who is trained in general medicine
2	a consultant	b	medical treatment which involves cutting the body open
3	a general practitioner (GP)	c	the room in a hospital where operations are performed
4	an operating theatre	d	a senior hospital doctor who specialises in one area of medicine
5	to prescribe	e	to ask a doctor for information or advice
6	surgery (uncountable)	f	to tell a patient, usually in writing, what treatment or medicine to have
7	a surgery (countable)	g	a place where a doctor or dentist examines or treats patients

Listening 1

a Work with a partner and answer the following questions.

1 How long do you spend with your doctor when you go for a consultation?
2 Do you think doctors spend enough time with patients during a consultation?
3 Read the statement below. Can you tell what the speaker's attitude would be from these words alone? Why / Why not?

A twenty-minute consultation per patient is the norm.

b The sentences below could all be added to the statement above. Match each sentence (1–4) with the adjective (a–d) that describes what the sentence expresses.

1 So you needn't worry, Mrs Smith, you haven't taken up too much of my time.   a neutral

2 You wouldn't catch me spending that long discussing old Mr Taggart's diabetes with him.   b reassuring

3 Here in Britain, however, we average only six minutes per patient.   c enthusiastic

4 Now that's what we should be doing too!   d scornful

c ▣▣ You will hear the statement recorded four times, each time with a different intonation. For each sentence, choose an adjective (a–d) from **b** to describe the intonation.

Sentence 1 	Sentence 2 	Sentence 3 	Sentence 4 ....

exam tip

Sometimes multiple choice questions (Parts 1 and 3) or 'who said what' questions (Part 4) test your ability to recognise a speaker's **attitude** from his/her **intonation**.

Listening 2 `Exam task, Part 1`

◼️◼️ You will hear four different extracts. For questions **1–8**, choose the answer (**A**, **B** or **C**) which fits best according to what you hear.

Extract 1

You will hear a British GP talking to his wife about an international medical conference he has just attended.

1 What he enjoyed most about the conference was

   A listening to the talks.
   B socialising with other doctors.
   C learning about other people's attitudes to health care.

2 His description of typical German health complaints and cures is

   A slightly scornful.
   B neutral.
   C very enthusiastic.

Extract 2

You will hear a later part of the same conversation.

3 If a British patient is not prescribed medicine by his doctor he feels
   A anxious.
   B reassured.
   C disappointed.

4 Compared to British patients, French patients expect
   A more medicines and longer consultations.
   B more medicines but shorter consultations.
   C fewer medicines but longer consultations.

Extract 3

You will hear an extract from an interview with a consultant on the subject of obesity in children.

5 In the last ten years the number of overweight children in France and Greece
   A has risen by fifty per cent.
   B has doubled.
   C has reached the same proportion as in the United States.

6 The most serious problems caused by childhood obesity occur
   A in children under thirteen.
   B in children aged thirteen and over.
   C in later life.

Extract 4

You will hear another extract from the same interview.

7 What does the consultant say about take-away hamburgers?
   A They do no harm if eaten occasionally.
   B They are eaten too frequently.
   C They contain too much protein.

8 What worries her about the research carried out at Exeter University?
   A It was based on incorrect statistics.
   B The data it collected was inaccurate.
   C The findings were alarming.

Speaking A

Commenting on the photographs Interview, Part 2

Work with a partner. Look at photographs **2** and **5** and compare and contrast the people and activities shown.

Collaborative task Interview, Part 2

Work with a partner. Imagine that your local health authority is launching a campaign to raise awareness of how to bring up healthy children. Posters entitled, 'Their Future's in Your Hands' are to be distributed to waiting rooms in clinics, hospitals and doctors' surgeries. Talk about what aspects of children's health are illustrated by the photographs above, and decide which of these images should appear on the poster.

> **Useful words and phrases**
>
> chubby   apathetic   glowing with health   sedentary   vigorous   fit   junk food
> underweight babies   fresh food   nutrients   a vaccination   (to) jeopardise
> health education   (to) vaccinate against   (to) act as a role model   respiratory problems
> preventive measures
>
> Do you think the poster should present good models or examples of things to be avoided?
> I think this picture aims to show the long-term health benefits / risks of ..., such as ...
> These images concentrate on the things a parent can do to ...

Long turn Interview, Part 3

a Look at the prompt card below. The sentences below it make up a short talk based on this prompt card. Number them **1–16** in the order you would expect to hear them. Three have already been numbered to help you.

> To what extent are people responsible for their own health?
> ▶ hereditary influences
> ▶ environmental influences
> ▶ lifestyle and habits

For example, if you suffer from asthma, you can avoid going to smoky environments, like crowded cafés or pubs. (**9**)

But, in general, I would say people are not really responsible for health problems that are inherited. (**6**)

Several factors have to be considered when evaluating people's responsibility for their own health. (**1**)

Where lifestyle and habits are concerned, however, there is a lot that people can do to keep themselves healthy.

Short of moving house, there's not a lot you can do about that.

First of all, the hereditary influences.

They can make sure they have a healthy diet which contains plenty of fruit and vegetables and should make time in their lives for regular exercise.

I believe that some of these are under our own control.

It is well known that certain diseases, such as haemophilia, are inherited, and clearly this is not something you can alter.

Next, environmental influences.

Obviously, if you know this, you can take steps to reduce your chances of the illness actually developing.

On the other hand, if you live in a polluted environment, such as a congested city centre, or an area with a lot of factory emissions, you are bound to have a higher risk of developing breathing problems.

Recent research also shows that you can have a genetic predisposition towards certain illnesses or conditions, like cancer or asthma.

So to sum up, I think people are responsible for their own health where lifestyle and habits are concerned, but much less so when it comes to genetic and environmental influences.

So, on the whole, I'd say people are only partially responsible for environmental influences on their health.

They can also avoid bad habits, like smoking, and try to reduce stress in their lives.

b Note down phrases from the sentences in **a** that perform the functions below. Follow the examples.

introduce the whole talk	*Several factors have to be considered when …*
introduce the different points	
summarise the different points	*in general*
summarise the whole talk	
introduce examples	*for example*

c Work with a partner. Brainstorm ideas and examples for a talk based on this prompt card.

> To what extent are people healthier nowadays than a hundred years ago?
> ▶ diet
> ▶ infectious diseases
> ▶ physical activity

d Work with a different partner. Take turns to give a talk based on the prompt card in **c**. Use phrases from **b** to help you organise and structure your talk. When it is your turn to listen, tick (✓) any phrases from **b** that your partner uses.

Listening B

Before you listen

Choose words or phrases from the box to replace the words in bold in the sentences.

| administered | alleviated | degenerative | immune system |
| lethal | limbs | severed | side effects |

1 The nurse accidentally **gave the patient** such a high dose that it proved to be **the cause of his death**.

2 Towards the end of her life, the drugs no longer **reduced the intensity of** her pain.

3 She is suffering from paralysis of her **arms and her legs**.

4 He was rushed to the hospital because his hand had been **completely cut off**.

5 The disease this patient is suffering from is **going to get worse over time**.

6 AIDS is a disease which attacks your **body's processes which protect you against infection**.

7 The pills she took for her allergy had some **extra results which she didn't want**, such as making her feel sleepy.

Listening 1 | Exam task, Part 2

a 🔲 You will hear a news bulletin about microsurgery. For questions **1–9**, complete the sentences with a word or short phrase.

The first successful operation in [1] _____ to reconstruct a severed hand inspired the opening of a special centre for microsurgery.

Because operations of this type are very long, microsurgeons need to have a lot of [2] _____ .

Blood vessels are tiny, so great [3] _____ is needed when sewing them back together.

[4] _____ per cent of patients who've had a limb restored find it works almost as well as before it was severed.

The unusual feature about the operation performed in Lyons was that the hand that was reattached belonged to someone who was already [5] _____ .

Unlike organs, hands are seen as part of one's [6] _____ and so the doctors fear the patient may have psychological difficulty in accepting a new one.

All transplants carry a risk of [7] _____ .

To try and avoid this, drugs which [8] _____ the immune system are administered.

By taking these drugs, patients put themselves at [9] _____ of developing cancer.

b Now listen again and check, complete or amend your answers.

Listening 2 `Exam task, Part 3`

a ▣ You will hear a doctor talking about euthanasia. For questions **1–5**, choose the answer (**A**, **B**, **C** or **D**) which fits best according to what you hear.

1 The term 'voluntary euthanasia'

- **A** has been made up by the media.
- **B** refers to a licence that will permit doctors to assist a patient to die.
- **C** refers to who makes the decision to bring about death.
- **D** is synonymous with the term 'active euthanasia'.

[1]

2 The difference between active euthanasia and assisted suicide lies in

- **A** the fact that one is legal and the other is not.
- **B** whether it is a doctor or a nurse that is involved.
- **C** the method by which death is brought about.
- **D** who actually carries out the act that causes death.

[2]

3 If he disconnects a dying patient from a life support machine, a doctor

- **A** is performing passive euthanasia.
- **B** risks prosecution.
- **C** needn't get permission from a patient or his family.
- **D** prolongs the dying process.

[3]

4 By giving very high doses of painkillers, a doctor

- **A** is acting against the law.
- **B** is behaving unethically.
- **C** may speed up the dying process.
- **D** gets practical results.

[4]

5 Doctors who do, or would, perform euthanasia feel that

- **A** all terminally ill patients suffer unbearable pain.
- **B** pain relief is inadequate in terminal illness.
- **C** it is humane to help a terminally ill patient to die if he or she wants to.
- **D** if a person's body is destroyed by disease his or her life isn't worth living.

[5]

b Now listen again and check, complete or amend your answers.

Listening 3 `Exam task , Part 4`

a ▣ You will hear a conversation between two people. They are discussing a television programme on surrogate mothers. For questions **1–6**, decide whether the opinions are expressed by only one of the speakers, or whether the speakers agree.

Write: Ⓛ for Louise, Ⓙ for Joe or Ⓑ for both, where they agree.

1 It is right to ban financial surrogacy agreements. ☐
2 The surrogate called Sandy may not have been honest about her intentions. ☐
3 Surrogate mothers sometimes change their minds about giving up the child. ☐
4 Acting as a surrogate mother should be done in a professional manner. ☐
5 Compassion ought to be the main motive for becoming a surrogate. ☐
6 Doctors who assist at a birth should be paid for their services. ☐

b Now listen again and check, complete or amend your answers.

Speaking B

Commenting on the photographs Interview, Part 2

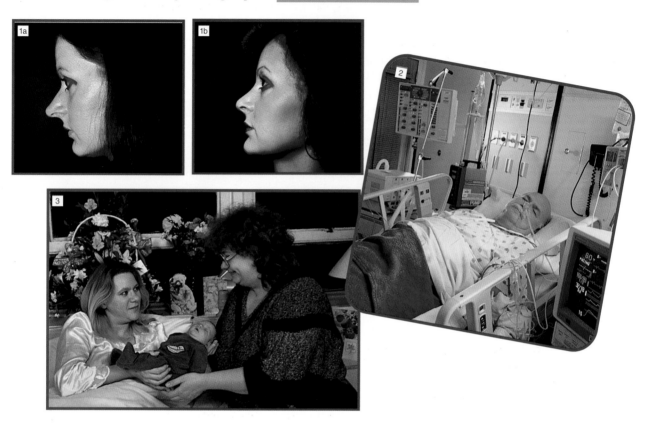

Work with a partner. Look at photographs **1a** and **1b**. Discuss in what way you think the woman's feelings about herself may be different in each photograph, and why.

Collaborative task Interview, Part 2

Work with a partner. Imagine that a magazine is publishing a feature entitled '*Medicine and Ethics*' and is considering using these photographs to accompany the article. Talk together about what aspect of medicine and ethics each photograph might depict, then decide which would be appropriate to include with the article. If you think none of these photographs would be particularly suitable, suggest alternative images which would be more appropriate.

> **Useful words and phrases**
>
> a nose job   cosmetic surgery   a heart monitor   diagnostic equipment
> a surrogate mother   (to) be/have reconstructed
> (to) enhance someone's looks   (to) prolong life/pain/suffering
> (to) improve upon nature   (to) interfere with the course of nature
> (to) let nature take its course   (to) overcome fertility problems
>
> In my view, the purpose of medicine is(n't) to …
> A doctor's role should(n't) be to …
> This image raises the question of how ethical it is …
> I don't think this picture is particularly relevant because …

Discussion Interview, Part 3

a Look at the discussion question and the points below it. Mark the points which support the proposition in the question **for**, and those which support the opposite viewpoint **against**.

> **Has modern medicine created more problems than it has solved?**

> **a** antibiotics can control diseases that used to kill
>
> **b** degenerative diseases and illnesses of the immune system are on the increase
>
> **c** dyslexia, autism and learning difficulties have been linked to vaccinations
>
> **d** increased longevity puts a huge burden on state health care and pension systems
>
> **e** infant mortality has decreased thanks to vaccinations
>
> **f** organ transplants give people a second lease of life
>
> **g** overuse of antibiotics has created antibiotic-resistant 'superbugs'
>
> **h** people live longer than before

b Work in two groups. One group brainstorms more ideas to support the proposition in the question. The other group thinks of extra ideas which are against the proposition.

> **exam tip**
>
> In the final discussion stage of the interview, the examiner will address questions to both candidates in general. If it's a difficult question and you need time to think, do not remain silent for a long time while you are thinking. Try using 'fillers' like:
>
> *That's an interesting question.*
> *Well, it's not something I've thought about a lot, but I would say …*

c Work with a partner from the opposite group to the one you were in when doing task **b**.
Discuss the question in **a**. Begin your discussion immediately after your teacher reads the question aloud.

> **Useful phrases**
>
> Yes, on the whole, I think it has. Take the question/problem of … , for example.
> No, I couldn't agree with that at all. I mean, just think of …
> I wouldn't say it's created more than it's solved, but it certainly isn't perfect.
> Yes, but you've got to remember that …
> I take your point about …, but you also have to take the fact that … into account.
> I'm not so sure about that. It seems to me that …
> Well, you may be right where … is concerned, but what about …?
> I'm sorry, but I don't quite understand the point you're making here.
> OK, to put it in other words, …

The consumer society

Listening A

Think about the topic

1 Do you regard shopping as a chore or a pleasure?

2 How easily influenced are you by advertising?

Before you listen

Complete the gaps in the short text below with the words and phrases in the box.

basic necessities	brand	chains	economies of scale	exploit
fair trade practices	groceries	growers	merchandise	retailers	suppliers

If supermarkets support **1** ...., they agree to pay a fair price to the **2** ....

or **3** .... who produce food, and to avoid sources which **4** .... workers or

farmers. Supermarket **5** .... have such a high turnover of goods that the

6 .... allow them to offer their **7** .... at prices below that of smaller

8....................... . In many cases, they also sell **9** .... such as **10** .... and

household goods, under their own **11** ....

Listening 1 Exam task, Part 2

a ▭▭ You will hear an appeal from a charity. For questions **1–9**, complete the sentences with a word or short phrase.

Much of the fruit we eat has been ◻**1**_____ by people whose lives are very hard.

Benedicto ties up banana trees both ◻**2**_____ attending school each day.

His hourly ◻**3**_____ is equivalent to the cost of one canned soft drink from the plantation shop.

It is only thanks to his ◻**4**_____ that Benedicto and his brothers can afford to go to school.

Employers like children as a source of ◻**5**_____ because they do not question the working hours.

Consumers are beginning to be aware of the ◻**6**_____ that is often involved in food production.

As a result, they are exerting ◻**7**_____ on supermarkets to adopt fair trade practices.

This means that supermarkets are now signing agreements that they won't buy goods unless the people who produce them work in ◻**8**_____ .

In addition, by paying fair prices, the need for ◻**9**_____ to work should be eliminated.

b Now listen again and check, complete or amend your answers.

Listening 2 Exam task, Part 4

a 〔⬛⬛〕 You will hear part of a conversation between two friends, Adrian and Norma. They are discussing a supermarket chain called Rosebury's, which offers a number of extra services. For questions **1–6**, decide whether the opinions are expressed by only one of the speakers, or whether the speakers agree.

Write: (A) for Adrian, (N) for Norma or (B) for both, where they agree.

* An Internet Service Provider (ISP) is a company which enables its customers to connect their computers to the Internet via a phone line.

1 ISPs do not necessarily make a lot of money.

2 The more people shop online, the more profitable it will become.

3 Rosebury's Internet service may appeal to people who are not very computer literate.

4 Many people prefer to deal with organisations they are already familiar with.

5 Rosebury's delivery service is good value for money.

6 Supermarkets are trying hard to make shopping more convenient.

b Now listen again and check, complete or amend your answers.

Listening 3 Exam task, Part 3

a 〔⬛⬛〕 You will hear an interview with a compulsive shopper. For questions **1–5**, choose the answer (**A**, **B**, **C** or **D**) which fits best according to what you hear.

1 Compulsive shoppers

  A suffer more than other people from anxiety and depression.
  B use shopping as a way of altering their mood.
  C are usually disappointed later with the goods they have bought.
  D usually buy exclusive goods for themselves.

  `1`

2 An addiction to shopping

  A is very common in women.
  B can afflict both men and women.
  C affects a high percentage of the British population.
  D is largely imaginary.

  `2`

3 Compulsive shoppers

  A harm nobody but themselves.
  B frequently have a lot of credit cards.
  C value money more than personal relationships.
  D may be unscrupulous about whose money they use.

  `3`

4 When he first found out how much Shelley had spent, her husband

  A was furious.
  B was shocked.
  C suggested that she needed professional help.
  D asked for a divorce.

  `4`

5 Shelley's counselling

  A showed her that society was to blame for her compulsion.
  B gave her self-confidence.
  C covered psychological and practical issues.
  D gave her the chance to talk about her problems.

  `5`

b Now listen again and check, complete or amend your answers.

Speaking A

Commenting on the photographs Interview, Part 2

```
BUY NOTHING DAY
   Nov 24, 2001
---------------------
No Purchase Necessary
---------------------
Consumer        0.00
Gr£ed           0.00
I$              0.00
Killing         0.00
Our             0.00
Plan£t          0.00

Total:          0.00
---------------------
  THANK YOU FOR
  NOT SHOPPING
---------------------
www.buynothingday.co.uk
```

What do you think the artist's purpose was in creating these images?

Collaborative task Interview, Part 2

Work with a partner. Imagine that you are organising a protest against consumerism. This will take the form of a 'Buy Nothing Day' on which you try to encourage people not to purchase anything inessential. These pictures show a poster and a mock receipt which have been used on Buy Nothing Days in Britain. Discuss what issues each piece of artwork raises and how appropriate these images and ideas would be for an event of this type in the country where you live.

Useful words and phrases

greed   consumerism   carrier bags   excessive packaging   consumer durables
compulsive shopping   (to) publicise   (to) draw someone's attention to
a clever gimmick   (to) reduce spending   (to) be taken in by advertising
(to) create demand   (to) combat the system   globalisation
(to) think twice about what you purchase

I think what the maker of these images is trying to say is ...
This campaign was obviously devised to ...
Do you think this idea would be popular in ...?
I don't agree entirely with ...
While I can see the point they are trying to make ...
I couldn't agree with you more.

Long turn Interview, Part 3

a Work in groups of three or four students. Together, brainstorm some ideas for each of the three points on the prompt card below.

> In what ways can the consumer society be harmful?
> ▶ environmental effects
> ▶ economic effects
> ▶ consumers' health and wellbeing

b Now work with a partner who was in a different group. Take turns to give your talk. When you are the listener:

- Make a note of the time your partner starts his/her talk and when he/she finishes it.

- If he/she continues for substantially longer than two minutes, interrupt him/her by raising your hand.

- At the end of his/her talk inform him/her what you liked about his/her talk.

- Tell him/her what you agree/disagree with that he/she said.

- Inform him/her how long exactly he/she spoke for.

exam tip

It is important to have a feeling for how long a two-minute talk lasts, so that you don't speak for substantially too long during the long turn in the interview, or run out of things to say before the time is up. Either of these faults will lose you marks for discourse management (see Exam factfile page 2). At home, try practising some talks based on prompt cards in the units you have studied so far, and time yourself while you do so.

Follow-up questions Interview, Part 3

Now work with a different partner and discuss these questions.

- Do you think children are bigger consumers than adults?
- How popular is online shopping in the country where you live?
- Do compulsive shoppers deserve our contempt or our sympathy?
- How far does having lots of possessions contribute to personal happiness?

Listening B

Before you listen

a Work with a partner. What methods are used in your country to advertise the products below? Write the words and phrases in the box in the correct part of the chart.

> **alcoholic drinks**   **canned soft drinks**   **computer games**   **CDs and cassettes**
> **chocolates and sweets**   **cigarettes**   **teen fashions**   **toys**

Advertising method/channel	Products
Ads on buses, trains etc	
Billboards and posters	
Magazines	
Sports sponsorship	
TV and Radio	

b Match the words (**1–3**) with the definition (**a–c**).

1	impulse purchase	**a**	a company's special colours
2	livery	**b**	a company's or product's symbol
3	logo	**c**	a thing you buy on the spur of the moment

Listening 1

◼️◼️ You will hear three different extracts. For questions **1–6**, choose the answer (**A, B** or **C**) which fits best according to what you hear.

Extract 1

You will hear a radio discussion about sponsorship of Formula 1 racing.

1 The presenter feels that

A he's too old to appreciate Formula 1.
B Formula 1 was more exciting in the old days.
C sponsorship of Formula 1 racing is too blatant.

`1`

2 Tobacco companies hope that

A people will associate their products with the excitement of racing.
B men will associate smoking cigarettes with having fun.
C smokers will switch to their brand if it's advertised on cars.

`2`

Extract 2

You will hear a discussion between a woman and her son.

3 What do the boy and his mother disagree about?

A The amount of television he and his sister should watch.
B The amount of influence TV ads may have on his sister.
C The amount of influence parents can have on children's buying habits.

`3`

4 The research the boy quotes concluded that advertising

A can be damaging to children.
B has little or no effect on children.
C may be beneficial.

`4`

Extract 3

You will hear part of a lecture given to first-year university students on a marketing course.

5 Women treasure possessions that

    A make them look nice.

    B have sentimental value.

    C they have had for a long time.

| 5 |

6 Men make impulse purchases if they see something

    A they think is good quality.

    B that will help them to pursue a favourite hobby.

    C that they feel reflects their individuality.

| 6 |

---

exam tip

Sometimes a listening passage may be on a topic about which you are well-informed. Remember that the exam tests your listening skills, not your general knowledge or ideas.

- Do not allow your own knowledge or opinions to interfere.
- Base your answers only on what you hear.

Listening 2   Exam task, Part 2

a 🔊 You will hear another, longer extract from the lecture you heard in Listening 1, Extract 3. For questions **1–9**, complete the sentences with a word or short phrase.

Advertisements show that men are much more interested in their

| 1 | than they used to be.

The pictures you see in advertisements are not realistic, but present

| 2 | images for people to emulate.

Ads aimed at women imply that by making themselves feel happy, they will be

| 3 | by men.

The terms 'precision', 'performance' and 'power' frequently appear in the text and/or the

| 4 | of ads aimed at men.

Many ads imply that a man and his potential purchase share the same

| 5 | .

Women in ads are frequently shown | 6 | .

Recently, ads have started promoting | 7 | for men.

Like those aimed at women, these ads play on people's desire to be

| 8 | to the opposite sex.

However, if the ad is targeted at a male audience, it usually includes

| 9 | in the photograph.

b Now listen again and check, complete or amend your answers.

Speaking B

Commenting on the photographs Interview, Part 2

Work with a partner. Look at all the images and decide what common theme binds most of them and if there are any which do not fit with this theme.

Collaborative task Interview, Part 2

Work with a partner. Imagine that you live in a country which, so far, has absolutely no controls on what products may be advertised or how they may be advertised. You have been asked to advise the government on what controls should be introduced to protect people from being influenced too much by advertisements. Talk together about which methods you think are appropriate or inappropriate for advertising the products shown in the picture(s) and decide what controls you would impose.

> **exam tip**
>
> Remember to listen carefully to the instructions for the collaborative task, and to keep your discussion relevant to what you have been asked to do. For example, you might feel that all advertising is immoral, but this is not what you have been asked to discuss. Nor should you let a discussion about cigarette advertisements diverge into a debate about the dangers of passive smoking.

Useful words and phrases

underage children   vulnerable members of the public   easily influenced
(to) ban   (to) forbid   (to) permit   (to) expose someone to something
potentially harmful   create the impression (that)   prime time TV
magazines/advertisements aimed at   (to) restrict/be restricted to

I think we're getting a bit off the point here.
That's an interesting idea/point/view, but I don't think it's entirely relevant to the question of ...
That's true, but perhaps we should come back to what we were saying about ...

Discussion Interview, Part 3

a Look at these two statements and decide which you would tend to agree with more.

> **Advertising reflects the real world.**

> **Advertising shapes the real world.**

b Form a group with other people who agree with the same statement as you. Brainstorm ideas to support your argument. Consider the areas below. You may also want to refer to examples of well-known current or recent advertisements to back up your arguments.

- the way people look
- the things people want to buy
- the things people need to buy
- the things people want to do with their lives
- people's habits and lifestyles
- other (your ideas)

c Now find a partner from the other group. Discuss the points in **a**, using the ideas and examples you came up with in **b**.

Long turn Interview, Part 3

Find a different partner to the one you had in the activities above. Take turns to give a short talk based on the prompt card below. Use any relevant ideas that came up during the group brainstorming or in the course of discussion with your previous partner.

To what extent does advertising reflect the real world?
▶ standards of physical attractiveness
▶ hopes and aspirations
▶ lifestyles

exam tip

The bullet points given on the prompt card are there to help you come up with and organise some ideas. However, you do not have to include all, or indeed any, of them if you don't want to. If you have plenty of ideas of your own that are **relevant to the topic,** talk about these instead.

Useful phrases

On the whole, ...   In general, ...   Generally speaking, ...   By and large, I would say ...
... barely reflect(s)/mirror(s) reality/the real world at all.
... presents a fairly realistic/somewhat idealised/totally unrealistic view of ...
... bears little/some/considerable resemblance to ...
This is particularly true of ...
However, where ... is concerned, ...
This is even more/far less apparent if you consider ...

Crime and punishment

Listening A

Think about the topic

Work with a partner and discuss the following questions.

1 What makes people commit crimes?

2 Should all police officers carry guns? Why? / Why not?

3 Would you enjoy serving on a jury? Why? / Why not?

Before you listen

Match the words and phrases (**1–10** and **a–i**) to make common word combinations.
Two items in the column on the left can go with one of the phrases **a–i**. Use a dictionary
to check the meanings if necessary.

1	to commit	**a**	on the run
2	to go	**b**	a crime *or* an offence
3	to be sought	**c**	of theft
4	to restrain	**d**	for questioning
5	to be arrested	**e**	a violent suspect
6	to be accused	**f**	a sentence
7	to be alleged	**g**	to have stolen a diamond ring
8	to be convicted	**h**	a criminal record
9	to serve	**i**	for fraud
10	to have		

Listening 1

🔲 You will hear an extract from a news bulletin about the use of CS spray by the British
police. For questions **1–2**, choose the answer (**A**, **B** or **C**) which fits best according to what
you hear.

1 What differentiates the British police from police in most other countries?

A They carry firearms only in special circumstances.

B They use short sticks known as truncheons. `1`

C They use CS spray if suspects resist arrest.

2 What is the police's view of CS spray?

A It is perfectly safe.

B It is the only viable alternative to guns. `2`

C Its use has prevented deaths during arrests.

Listening 2

a 📼 You will hear a news bulletin about a mother and son who are both criminals. For questions **1–7**, complete the sentences with one or two words, or a short phrase.

The mother and son team were caught while attempting to carry out an act

of [**1**].

The police found a passport belonging to a missing woman in the suspects'

[**2**].

They were also carrying a gun, several suspicious documents and a large quantity of

[**3**] in a stolen car.

The pair are thought to have [**4**] and possibly murdered several of the

people named in the documents.

Police in Las Vegas suspect the mother and son of having burnt down a house in order to make a false

[**5**] claim.

Various police forces had [**6**] the pair's movements, but had been

unable to catch them.

The woman had spent time in prison after being [**7**] of enslavement.

b Now listen again and check, complete or amend your answers.

Listening 3 | Exam task, Part 3

a 📼 You will hear a radio programme about the use of closed circuit televisions (CCTVs).
For questions **1–5**, choose the answer (**A**, **B**, **C** or **D**) which fits best according to what you hear.

1 The reporter thinks that
   A a novelist's predictions are coming true.
   B her every move is being watched.
   C all public places should have CCTVs.
   D the authorities are watching people by means of hidden cameras.

2 Norman Clark thinks that CCTV is
   A effective in preventing crime.
   B effective in detecting crime.
   C ineffective in preventing and detecting crime.
   D less effective than is generally believed.

3 Research done on CCTV use shows that
   A the cameras watch people who are not criminals.
   B the resulting tapes are inadequately monitored.
   C very few arrests are made as a result of recording people.
   D professional criminals know how to avoid the cameras.

4 The reporter thinks that the use of CCTV
   A saves money for the police.
   B leads to blackmail.
   C provides useful evidence for use in trials.
   D should be controlled by law.

5 In general, the reporter's attitude to the way CCTV is used is
   A angry.
   B neutral.
   C concerned.
   D paranoid.

b Now listen again and check, complete or amend your answers.

Speaking A

Commenting on the photographs Interview, Part 2

Work with a partner. Look at photographs **1** and **5** and discuss what you think might have happened before the photos were taken.

Collaborative task Practice 2, Part 2

Work with a partner. Imagine that you are police officers working in an area of high crime, but where relations between the police and the local community are not good. As part of a drive to improve these relations, you have been asked to give a talk and slide show to pupils at the local secondary school. Talk about the photographs and decide what aspects of police work each illustrates, whether it should be included in the talk and what other photographs would be helpful to accompany the talk.

Useful words and phrases

scene of the crime   (to) investigate a murder   (to) collect evidence   (to) take fingerprints
(to) look for clues   a policeman on patrol   (to) arrest a suspect   (to) test someone for drink-driving
(to) drink and drive   alcohol in the blood   irresponsible behaviour   (to) fight crime
(to) raise public awareness of

Bear in mind that police relations with the community are …

These pictures are supposed to improve relations with the public so …

Are you sure that this picture would convey a positive message?

Well, you may be right that …

One important image that is missing here is …

One aspect of police work which should be included is …

Long turn Interview, Part 3

a In pairs look at the two prompt cards. Each of you should choose one to talk about.

Prompt card a

> What social changes can increasing crime rates be
> attributed to?
>
> ▶ family relationships
> ▶ economic factors
> ▶ demographic factors

Prompt card b

> To what extent should young people who commit crimes
> be held responsible for their actions?
>
> ▶ parental influences
> ▶ education
> ▶ peer pressure

b Without taking time to prepare, take turns to talk for up to two minutes about the topic you have chosen. When you are the listener, make a note of the time your partner speaks for and the main ideas he/she puts over in the talk. Did he/she manage to speak for about two minutes? Did he/she say something about all three points on the card?

c Now form a group with the other students who talked about the same prompt card as you. In your group put together some ideas about the prompt card which you did **not** speak about earlier.

d Find a different partner from the opposite group and take turns to give your second talk. Were you able to talk for the full two minutes this time?

exam tip

In the interview, you will have no more than ten seconds to think about what you want to say in the long turn. It is very important, therefore, that you should already have a fund of ideas and opinions about a wide range of topics of contemporary interest. The themes covered in this book, and in your other textbooks, give a guide to the type of topics that may come up in the interview. Remember, however, that your talk should relate specifically to the question on the prompt card, so do not prepare speeches by heart.

Discussion Interview, Part 3

Work in groups of two or three people. Discuss the questions below.

- Do you think enough is done to help the victims of crime?
- To what extent can members of the public help to prevent crimes?
- What can be done to reduce juvenile crime?
- Should members of the public be allowed to carry firearms for purposes of self-defence?

Listening B

Before you listen

Match the words and phrases (**1–9**) with the correct definitions (**a–i**).

1	bail	**a**	be kept in prison while awaiting trial
2	be on remand	**b**	change the punishment given to a criminal to one that is less severe
3	beyond redemption		
4	commute a sentence	**c**	compulsory
5	a defendant	**d**	help someone to live a useful life again after they have been in prison
6	an inmate		
7	mandatory	**e**	money left with a court to prove that the accused will return when the trial starts
8	rehabilitate	**f**	someone who is kept in a prison
9	a whole-life sentence	**g**	the person in a court of law who has been accused of doing something illegal
		h	the punishment of keeping someone in prison until they die
		i	too bad to be saved or improved

Listening 1

◼◼ You will hear two different extracts. For questions **1–4**, choose the answer (**A**, **B** or **C**) which fits best according to what you hear.

Extract 1

You will hear a woman talking about an incident that happened in a courtroom.

1 The woman is describing

   A watching a trial.
   B giving evidence in court.
   C being a member of a jury.

   `1`

2 She and the other women felt nervous because

   A they had never been in this situation before.
   B they thought they might be robbed.
   C they were worried that the defendants' friends would try to intimidate them.

   `2`

Extract 2

You will hear a discussion about a project for prison inmates.

3 What is the ultimate goal of the project the woman is working on?

   A To educate prison inmates.
   B To save taxpayers' money.
   C To prevent convicted criminals from re-offending.

   `3`

4 What do the man and woman agree about?

   A The usefulness of the project.
   B The link between unemployment and crime.
   C The fact that many former prison inmates commit further crimes.

   `4`

Listening 2 Exam task, Part 4

a ⬛ You will hear two friends, Tom and Kate, discussing how murderers should be dealt with. For questions **1–6**, decide whether the opinions are expressed by only one of the speakers, or whether the speakers agree.

Write: (T) for Tom, (K) for Kate or (B) for both, where they agree.

> **exam tip**
>
> Note that you are asked to identify opinions **expressed** by the speakers. Do not confuse these with other people's opinions which are **reported** by the speakers.

1 Lord Bingham is more liberal than other judges. ☐
2 A whole-life sentence may be appropriate in some cases. ☐
3 Prison sentences fail to rehabilitate criminals. ☐
4 You can never be sure that violent criminals have mended their ways. ☐
5 Murderers are not let out of prison if the authorities think they will re-offend. ☐
6 The purpose of a whole-life sentence is to protect the public. ☐

b Now listen again and check, complete or amend your answers.

Listening 3 Exam task, Part 2

a ⬛ You will hear a radio programme cautioning travellers to Thailand about the risks of breaking the law there. For questions **1–9**, complete the sentences with one or two words, or a short phrase.

Some tourists attempt to enliven their holidays in Thailand by getting involved with [1 _____] .

The majority of British people in jail in Thailand are [2 _____] who have been given sentences of twenty-five years or more.

The death sentence is mandatory for people who are caught with one hundred grams of [3 _____] which they intend to sell.

For westerners, the punishment for this crime is reduced to a sentence lasting [4 _____] .

Many prisoners spend a long time on remand and [5 _____] is usually refused.

A suspect's best chance of getting a shorter sentence is by [6 _____] at all stages of the legal procedure.

As foreign prisoners have no [7 _____] to bring them blankets, food or money, they suffer even more than Thai ones.

Because of the very [8 _____] conditions in Thai prisons, many prisoners, especially foreign ones, are in poor health.

Although British prisoners may transfer to a British jail after four to eight years, they must still [9 _____] the same number of years in prison as they would have done in Thailand.

b Now listen again and check, complete or amend your answers.

Speaking B

Commenting on the photographs Interview, Part 2

Work with a partner. Look at photographs **1** and **4** and discuss what you think may be happening or about to happen in each picture.

Collaborative task Interview, Part 2

Work with a partner. Imagine that a law student is doing a project entitled 'Prison – The New School of Crime' and is looking for photographs to illustrate it. Discuss together what aspects of this topic each picture might illustrate and whether there are any other images that might also be appropriate.

> ### Useful words and phrases
>
> (to) grab   (to) snatch   (to) hold up   a balaclava   (to) be inside   (to) reoffend
> (to) be locked up   (to) appear in court   (to) graduate from one crime to another
> (to) learn new tricks of the trade   (to) make new contacts in the criminal world
>
> Perhaps we should discuss the project theme first. What do you understand by …?
> I think it relates to the fact that …
> In that case, which of these pictures conveys that idea?
> It's not entirely clear from the picture, but he seems to be holding …
> He looks as if he's …
> He might be about to …
> He obviously doesn't want to be recognised, so I think it's more likely that …

Long turn and follow-up Interview, Part 3

a Look at the two prompt cards below and decide quickly which one you would prefer to talk about. Then find a partner who has chosen the other card.

Prompt card a

To what extent have attitudes towards people who break the law changed in the last hundred years?
▶ penalties
▶ prison conditions
▶ public sympathy

Prompt card b

To what extent is the prison system effective?
▶ punishment
▶ rehabilitation
▶ protection of the public

b Take turns to give your talk to each other.
At the end of talk **a** the listener answers this question
Is there anything you don't agree with?

At the end of talk **b** the listener answers this question
Is there anything you would like to add?

c With your partner, discuss these questions.
What kind of problems do ex-prisoners face once they have been released from jail?
Do you think the death penalty should be reinstated for certain crimes?

exam tip

All the interview materials are there to generate discussion. Remember that:
• there are no 'right' or 'wrong' answers.
• you will not lose marks in the exam if you have unusual opinions or unconventional ideas.

So go ahead and say what you want to say – the important thing is to communicate.

Discussion Interview, Part 3

Discuss these questions in small groups.

• Are there any circumstances in which someone would be justified in taking the law into their own hands?
• Do you believe that nobody is beyond redemption?
• Does crime ever pay?

Useful phrases

justice has not been done   (to) feel let down by the law   (to) seek retribution
(to) take revenge on someone for something   (to) mend your ways
fundamentally evil/good   (to) give someone a second chance
(to) have something on your conscience   (to) feel pangs of conscience
in the short/long term

Art and heritage

Listening A

Think about the topic

1 What types of visual art do you enjoy?

2 What methods, if any, have been used to teach you to create or appreciate art?

3 What is the difference between 'heritage' and 'an inheritance'?

Before you listen

Match the words (**1–6**) with the correct definitions (**a–f**).

1	a crucifix	**a**	a flat board used by a painter to mix colours *or* the range of colours used by a painter in his/her work
2	a landscape		
3	a palette	**b**	a painting of inanimate objects, such as flowers and fruit, etc.
4	a portrait	**c**	a cross with a figure of Christ on it
5	a sculpture	**d**	a drawing, painting or photograph of a specific person
6	a still life	**e**	a drawing or painting showing a scene in the countryside
		f	a three-dimensional work of art made from stone, clay, plaster, bronze, etc.

Listening 1

▢▢ You will hear two extracts from an interview with the director of a private art school.
For questions **1–4**, choose the answer (**A**, **B** or **C**) which fits best according to what you hear.

Extract 1

1 Few people really see things because

  A they watch too much TV.
  B they are uninterested in simple objects.
  C they are overwhelmed by visual stimuli.

2 Some of the woman's students

  A find her classes don't fulfil their expectations.
  B already have a good eye for detail.
  C are learning to draw as a form of therapy.

Extract 2

3 Post-Impressionist and Expressionist paintings are characterised by

  A their use of strong geometric forms.
  B the wide brushstrokes used when painting them.
  C their brightness and variety of colours.

4 It's impossible to say how long it takes to learn to paint well because

  A everyone learns at a different pace.
  B few people bother to paint easily recognisable objects.
  C there's no agreed standard by which to judge someone's painting.

Listening 2

a 🔊 You will hear a lecturer talking about a painting known as *The Ambassadors* by the German painter Hans Holbein the Younger. For questions **1–9**, complete the notes about different objects in the painting with one or two words, a figure or date, or a short phrase.

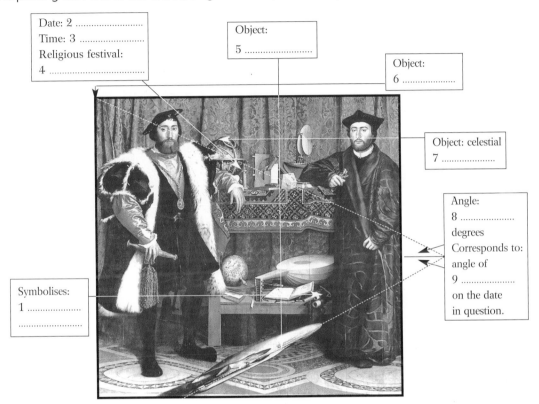

Date: 2 ....
Time: 3 ....
Religious festival:
4 ....

Object:
5 ....

Object:
6 ....

Object: celestial
7 ....

Angle:
8 .... degrees
Corresponds to:
angle of
9 ....
on the date
in question.

Symbolises:
1 ....

b Now listen again and check, complete or amend your answers.

Listening 3 Exam task, Part 3

a 🔊 You will now hear a different lecturer talking about the same painting as in Listening 2. For questions **1–5**, choose the answer (**A, B, C** or **D**) which fits best according to what you hear.

1 Oil paintings are special in that
  A they make objects look real.
  B they make you want to touch them.
  C they are based on illusions.
  D they are more colourful than sculptures.
  [1]

2 Holbein's painting of *The Ambassadors*
  A was created using real materials.
  B was created by craftsmen then completed by Holbein.
  C appeals to more than one sense.
  D cost a lot of money to produce.
  [2]

3 The function of oil painting was
  A to illustrate a break with previous traditions.
  B to link wealth with social status.
  C to show that it was socially acceptable to be rich.
  D to show what could be bought by the rich.
  [3]

4 The distorted skull
  A was painted using a mirror.
  B imparts a philosophical message.
  C should have been painted in the same way as the rest of the picture.
  D is utterly insignificant.
  [4]

5 The ambassadors
  A felt at ease with the painter.
  B wanted to keep a distance between each other.
  C wanted to be compared to kings and emperors.
  D wanted to appear both unique and reserved.
  [5]

b Now listen again and check, complete or amend your answers.

Speaking A

Commenting on the photographs Interview, Part 2

Work with a partner. Look at photograph **2** and discuss what you think is going on, and who would be interested in attending such an event.

Collaborative task Interview, Part 2

Work with a partner. Imagine that a philanthropist and arts lover has donated a substantial amount of money to the council in the town where you live, to raise local people's awareness and appreciation of visual art. A number of activities and excursions have already been proposed, as shown in the photographs. Talk together about the appropriacy of each proposal and suggest some alternative or additional activities.

> **Useful words and phrases**
>
> a still life   amateur/Sunday painters   an easel   a watercolour
> subdued lighting   a hushed/reverential atmosphere   a sense of awe/curiosity
> (to) scrutinise   (to) contemplate an auction   an auctioneer   an investment
> (to) go under the hammer   (to) bid for an original work of art   a solitary activity
> (to) feel the tension rising   (to) require concentration   a potter's wheel   clay
> kiln   (to) fire a pot
>
> We should perhaps think about the kind of people who live here before we …
> This might have a quite wide/rather narrow appeal, as …
> I'm not sure how far doing this would lead to an increased …
> Perhaps something a bit more … would be more appropriate for that age group.

Long turn and follow-up Interview, Part 3

exam tip

The materials you will be shown in the interview (photographs and prompt cards) do not include written instructions for the tasks you have to carry out. It is very important therefore that you are sure what you have to do. Ask the examiner for clarification:

- if you have not understood exactly what you have been asked to do, e.g.
  Sorry, but do you want me to answer that question, or would you like us to discuss it together?
- if you are not entirely sure what aspect of a topic you are meant to talk about, e.g.
  The prompt card mentions 'success'. Should I interpret that as having successfully mastered the art form, or as recognition and financial success?

a Look at the two prompt cards below and decide quickly which one you would prefer to talk about. Then find a partner who has chosen the other card.

Prompt card a

Should art and music be given more importance in the school curriculum?

- ▶ vocational skills
- ▶ personal development
- ▶ school budget

Prompt card b

Are painting and sculpture outdated as means of artistic expression?

- ▶ video
- ▶ advertising
- ▶ graffiti

b Take turns to give your talk to each other. At the end of each talk, the listener answers one of these questions.

- *Is there anything you don't agree with?*
- *Is there anything you would like to add?*
- *What do you think?*
- *How does this differ from your experience?*

c With your partner, discuss these questions.

- *Should training in some form of creative art be mandatory for all children?*
- *Should artists be subsidised, either by their families or by the state?*

Discussion Interview, Part 3

Work with a different partner. Discuss the points below.

- To what extent have writers and artists shaped our culture?
- Is art just an investment for the rich?
- What would make art galleries/museums more attractive to the general public?

Listening B

Before you listen

a Match the words (**1–4**) with the correct definitions (**a–d**).

1 a cast

2 a frieze

3 an inscription

4 a statute

a a formal rule of an institution or organisation

b a model of something made by pouring liquid, such as plaster, into a mould of the original object

c a piece of writing carved on a stone, in the front of a book, etc.

d a thin border along the top of the wall of a building, usually decorated with pictures or patterns

Listening 1 Exam task, Part 2

a ◨◧ You will hear part of a radio programme about the sculptures from the Parthenon which are known in Britain as the Elgin Marbles. They are now in the British Museum. For questions **1–9**, complete the sentences with one or two words, or a short phrase.

In a recent opinion poll, nearly forty percent of British people thought the marbles should be returned but almost **1** [   ] of the people asked had no opinion about the issue.

Elgin was given permission to remove the sculptures by the **2** [   ] of the Ottoman Empire.

The Parthenon had been badly damaged at the end of the seventeenth century during a **3** [   ] of Athens mounted by the Venetians.

Elgin claimed that his actions saved the marbles from possible **4** [   ] at the hands of the Turks.

However, some of his **5** [   ], including the poet Lord Byron, were highly critical of what he did.

It seems fairly clear that the Turks **6** [   ] Elgin's actions as a French diplomat was jailed for protesting about the removal of the marbles.

It also seems to be the case that Elgin did not **7** [   ] the sculptures.

However, in order to get the papers he needed, he may well have **8** [   ] large numbers of people.

Fifteen years after the plunder began, the whole collection was sold to **9** [   ].

b Now listen again and check, complete or amend your answers.

Listening 2 `Exam task, Part 3`

a 📼 The programme continues. For questions **1–5**, choose the answer (**A**, **B**, **C** or **D**) which fits best according to what you hear.

1 The main arguments concerning the ownership of the sculptures hinge on

   A whether Elgin really obtained permission from the Turks or not.

   B whether it was legal or not for the Turks to issue documents approving their removal.

   C whether Greece was an occupied country at the time or not.

   D whether it is legal or not for the British Museum to dispose of items in its collection.

1

2 The West frieze of the Parthenon

   A was in the British Museum until 1993.

   B suffered heavy damage from London's pollution.

   C was destroyed in the 1930s.

   D was copied by Elgin.

2

3 Lord Duveen, a millionaire art dealer

   A disagreed with scholars' opinions about the marbles.

   B planned to move the marbles to a new museum.

   C disliked the fact that the sculptures had been painted.

   D was unintentionally responsible for damage to the marbles.

3

4 Colin Forsyth thinks

   A Elgin's behaviour was morally reprehensible.

   B the question of legal ownership of the marbles is paramount.

   C Scottish art treasures should also be returned.

   D the Elgin Marbles should be returned to Greece.

4

5 Colin Forsyth thinks that if the marbles return to Greece

   A it may set off a chain reaction.

   B the British Museum will no longer appeal to visitors.

   C the Louvre will become the foremost international museum.

   D the British Museum will replace them with replicas.

5

b Now listen again and check, complete or amend your answers.

exam tip

In the exam, never leave a 'who said what' question (Part 4) or a multiple choice question (Parts 1 and 3) unanswered. Even if you take a guess, you stand a one in three or one in four chance of getting it right.

Listening 3 `Exam task, Part 4`

a 📼 You will hear a husband and wife, David and Liz, discussing their daughter and a pastime she is interested in. For questions **1–6**, decide whether the opinions are expressed by only one of the speakers, or whether the speakers agree.

Write: (D) for David, (L) for Liz or (B) for both, where they agree.

* Morris dances are traditional English country dances performed by men.

1 Not many young people are interested in traditional dances.

2 Their daughter will probably not become an outstanding dancer.

3 Parents should not make their children's achievements the focus of their own lives.

4 Knowing traditional dances can be a social asset.

5 Morris dancing can't be taken seriously.

6 Morris dancers' costumes originally had a practical purpose.

b Now listen again and check, complete or amend your answers.

Speaking B

Commenting on the photographs | Interview, Part 2

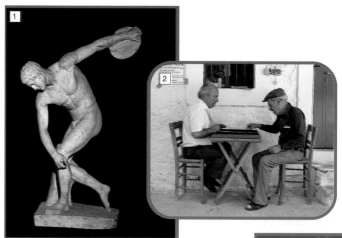

Work with a partner. Look at photographs **6** and **7** and discuss what you think might have happened before each photograph was taken.

Collaborative task | Practice 2, Part 2

Work with a partner. Imagine that you are assembling a pack of teaching materials to be used with pupils in junior high schools throughout the European Community. The objective of the pack is to stimulate discussion about Europe's heritage. The photos above may be included in the teaching pack. Talk together about what aspects of heritage each photo depicts and decide if any of the photographs are inappropriate and, if so, what image might be better to depict this idea.

Useful words and phrases

classical beauty   simplicity of form   backgammon   bagpipes   kilt
traditional/national dress   Gothic architecture   spire   illuminated
festive spirit   (to) have a nose for

Long turn and follow-up | Interview, Part 3

a Look at the two prompt cards below and decide quickly which one you would prefer to talk about. Then find a partner who has chosen the other card.

Prompt card a

To what extent does national heritage affect people's everyday lives?

▶ social customs

▶ family relationships

▶ leisure activities

Prompt card b

In what ways has the globalisation of culture diminished the role of national heritage?

▶ fashion

▶ art forms

▶ festivities

exam tip

In addition to the points about timing mentioned in Unit 6, page 47, your marks for *discourse management* will reflect your ability to link your ideas together logically with appropriate connecting words and phrases to show that you are moving from one point to the next, giving an example, expressing a personal opinion or a commonly-held opinion, highlighting an exception, etc.

Useful phrases

Undoubtedly, ...
This can be seen ...
However, where ... is concerned ...
The same can probably be said/not be said of ...
I think most people would agree that ...
When it comes to ...
This is clearly illustrated by the fact that ...
It's widely accepted that ...
In sharp contrast to this ...

b Take turns to give your talk to each other.
At the end of each talk, the listener answers one of these questions.

● *Is there anything you don't agree with?*
● *Is there anything you would like to add?*
● *What do you think?*
● *How does this differ from your experience?*

c With your partner, discuss these questions.

● *Is it appropriate nowadays to continue teaching children about their national heritage?*
● *Should internationally significant art treasures held in foreign museums be returned to their country of origin?*
● *To what extent does a national currency embody that country's heritage?*

Body and mind

Listening A

Think about the topic

1 What physical and mental preparation do athletes and sportspeople make?

2 Can you give any examples from your own experience of how mental preparation has helped your physical performance or vice versa?

3 What do you understand by the term 'nature versus nurture'?

Listening 1

 You will hear two extracts from an interview with a woman who has written a book about sumo wrestling. For questions **1–4**, choose the answer (**A**, **B** or **C**) which fits best according to what you hear.

Extract 1

1 The writer finds sumo interesting because

   A its champions are celebrities in Japan.
   B it embraces modern and ancient preoccupations.
   C it has religious significance.

                                     1

2 What is the interviewer's opinion of football players and fans?

   A They are irreligious.
   B They are under-educated.
   C They are badly-behaved.

                                       2

Extract 2

3 The author thinks that sumo wrestlers' size and weight

   A fascinates many people.
   B is more important than their skill.
   C is only achieved by rigorous training.

                                       3

4 The key to weight gain is

   A eating large amounts of food when very hungry.
   B drinking alcohol while eating large helpings of food.
   C sleeping immediately after eating copiously.

                                       4

exam tip

If you are hesitating between two possible answers to any question in the Listening paper during the exam:

- do not mark them both on the answer sheet. Even if one is correct, you will not be given marks for it.
- choose one or the other and hope that your decision is correct.

Listening 2 | Exam task, Part 2

a 📼 You will hear a radio programme about endurance sports. For questions **1–9**, complete
the notes with one or two words or a short phrase.

The endurance sport first tried by novices is the [1   ] .

Participants in the Hawaii Ironman triathlon included [2   ] .

One female endurance athlete ran non-stop [3   ] for over 13 days.

The challenge of endurance sports is compounded by doing them in

[4   ] .

The Deca Ironman takes place in a Mexican city which is [5   ] .

The distances in this contest are [6   ] times longer than in other
Ironman competitions.

Bob Brown suffered from hallucinations, as participants in Ironman contests do

not [7   ] .

Far from being [8   ] by his recent health problems, Brown is now
setting himself new, even harder, goals.

Bob Brown is so stimulated by the [9   ] of his sport that he
ignores its effects on his health.

b Now listen again and check, complete or amend your answers.

Listening 3 | Exam task, Part 3

a 📼 You will hear a radio interview about the use of performance-enhancing drugs in Olympic sports.
For questions **1–5**, choose the answer (**A**, **B**, **C** or **D**) which fits best according to what you hear.

1 The medal-winning swimmer was
suspended for
  A using performance-enhancing drugs.
  B refusing to provide a urine sample.
  C using banned substances.   [1]
  D interfering with a sample.

2 When Olympic champions are caught
using drugs, young athletes
  A feel cheated.
  B feel discouraged.
  C are tempted to do the same.   [2]
  D give up training.

3 Pat Delahaye
  A feels deeply humiliated.
  B will be publicly stripped of his
gold medals.
  C will have to undergo further drug tests.   [3]
  D has lost the respect of his supporters.

4 Pat Delahaye
  A was known to be using drugs
before the last Olympics.
  B was suspected of using drugs at
the time he won his gold medals.   [4]
  C improved his performance
through rigorous training.
  D was caught because drug tests
have become more effective.

5 The long-term effects of performance-
enhancing drugs
  A are as yet unknown.
  B are always fatal.
  C caused the early death of an
American runner.   [5]
  D have led to liver damage in large
numbers of athletes.

b Now listen again and check, complete or amend your answers.

Speaking A

Commenting on the photographs Interview, Part 2

Work with a partner. Look at photographs **2** and **3**. Discuss together how you think the people might be feeling and what you think might happen immediately after the moment captured in the photographs. You have about a minute for this.

Collaborative task Interview, Part 2

Work with a partner. A photographic exhibition is being organised on the theme of 'Mind Over Matter'. All these photographs are to be included. Talk together about which aspects of 'mind over matter' are being shown by the photographers. Then discuss two other angles on the topic which you think should be represented in the exhibition. You have about three minutes to talk about this.

> **Useful words and phrases**
> a specially-adapted wheelchair   glowing coals   a sculptured torso   bulging muscles
> on the verge of collapse   straining with effort/determination   drenched in sweat
> gleaming with oil   triumphant   a tremendous sense of achievement   tranquil
> oblivious to distractions/the outside world   (to) push oneself to the limit
> (to) refuse to accept defeat   (to) take pride in   (to) find inner peace

Long turn and follow-up Interview, Part 3

a Choose one of the prompt cards below. You have ten seconds to think briefly about the topic, then you should talk to the rest of the class for about two minutes. Your teacher will indicate when two minutes have passed, and give you feedback on your performance.

Prompt card a

To what extent do the modern Olympics embody the spirit of the ancient Olympic Games?
- ▶ drug scandals
- ▶ national pride
- ▶ financial rewards

Prompt card b

What functions does sport perform in people's lives nowadays?
- ▶ health
- ▶ social interaction
- ▶ challenge

Prompt card c

What should be borne in mind when bidding to host the Olympic Games?
- ▶ infrastructure
- ▶ security
- ▶ costs and revenue

b Listen carefully to the person who is talking. Your teacher will choose one person to answer a follow-up question on this talk. Your answer should last about a minute.

c Now work with a partner and discuss these questions. You have about one minute to discuss each question.

- ● *Would you ever risk your long-term health to pursue excellence in a sport?*
- ● *Should amateur sportsmen and sportswomen be allowed to accept money for sponsorship deals?*

Discussion Interview, Part 3

Work with a different partner. Choose one of the following questions to discuss together. Your discussion should last about three minutes. Your teacher will indicate when three minutes have passed. If you have run out of things to say before then, move on to one of the other questions.

- ● Is the desire to compete a healthy urge for society in general?
- ● How influential are successful sportspeople as role models?
- ● Is everyone motivated by challenges?

exam tip

Make sure before you go to your Proficiency speaking exam that you know exactly what will be expected of you at the different stages of the interview, and how long each part lasts. Look again at the Exam factfile, page 2, and Unit 1, pages 6, 7 and 11 to remind yourself of these points, if necessary.

Listening B

Listening 1

◨◨ You will hear two extracts. For questions **1–4**, choose the answer (**A**, **B** or **C**) which fits best according to what you hear.

Extract 1

You will hear a conversation at work between a man and a woman.

1 The man is worried about

   A giving a presentation.
   B attending a job interview.
   C asking his boss for a promotion.

                                                     1

2 The woman changed the man's attitude to the situation that was worrying him by

   A persuading him that there was nothing to worry about.
   B altering the way he thought about the problem.
   C comparing him to someone else who succeeded in a similar situation.

                                                     2

Extract 2

You will hear a telephone call between a young woman and her mother. They are discussing a form of exercise called Tai Chi.

3 According to the young woman, Tai Chi

   A discourages competitiveness.
   B is a mental and physical discipline.
   C teaches you self-control.

                                                     3

4 The girl thinks Tai Chi would improve her mother's

   A stress levels.
   B painful joints.
   C asthma.

                                                     4

Listening 2   Exam task, Part 4

a ◨◨ You will hear two people, Amanda and Mark, discussing talent and where it comes from. For questions **1–6**, decide whether the opinions are expressed by only one of the speakers, or whether the speakers agree.

Write: Ⓐ for Amanda, Ⓜ for Mark or Ⓑ for both, where they agree.

1 People place too much emphasis on the idea of innate talent.   ☐

2 Parental expectations shape the way a child's talent develops.   ☐

3 With encouragement and training, people can master a variety of skills   ☐

4 Genius is genetically determined.   ☐

5 People cannot influence the fact that they may have an inherited tendency towards getting certain illnesses.   ☐

6 The idea that intelligence is inherited is repugnant.   ☐

b Now listen again and check, complete or amend your answers.

Listening 3 Exam task, Part 3

a ▢ You will hear a radio programme about cloning. For questions **1–5**, choose the answer (**A**, **B**, **C** or **D**) which fits best according to what you hear.

1 Multiple clones of one person

    A could exist only in the realms of fiction.
    B could have anti-social tendencies.
    C would be identical in every respect.
    D would have different host mothers.

    1 ☐

2 Genetically engineering an underclass of manual workers would be

    A technically impossible.
    B environmentally unsound.
    C economically unfeasible.
    D exceedingly expensive.

    2 ☐

3 Professor Armstrong believes that in the future

    A most couples will be infertile.
    B people will customise the genes used for creating their offspring.
    C only the upper classes will choose to clone themselves.
    D cloning will become widely accepted.

    3 ☐

4 According to Professor Armstrong, the most difficult choice to make if cloning a human would be

    A which genetic characteristics it is ethical to enhance or eliminate.
    B whether it is ethical to eliminate the genes for illnesses which are inherited.
    C which aspects of character should be enhanced.
    D whether it is ethical to tamper with the genetic code of the clone at all.

    4 ☐

5 The technique of cloning could also be used

    A to create new cells.
    B to avoid the need for transplants.
    C to create new organs.
    D to prevent people dying of kidney disease.

    5 ☐

b Now listen again and check, complete or amend your answers.

Speaking B

Commenting on the photographs Interview, Part 2

Work with a partner. Look at photograph **3**. Discuss together what is happening in the picture and how the photograph makes you feel. You have about a minute for this.

Collaborative task Interview, Part 2

Imagine that an organisation which runs self-development courses is launching a new course entitled *'Unleash Your Hidden Potential'*. They are looking for an eye-catching image to include in their advertisement for the course. Talk together about how each of these photographs relates to the theme of the course and decide which of them would be the best to put in the advertisement. You have about three minutes to talk about this.

exam tip

Sometimes in the Interview there may not be an immediately recognisable link between the photographs and the task you have been asked to carry out. If this is the case:
- do not remain silent while you're thinking.
- do not just say bluntly *I can't see how this relates at all* or *I don't think any of these pictures are at all relevant to the topic.*
- use tentative language to express any possible links you can find (see useful words and phrases box below).
- ask your partner for his/her help and ideas.

Useful phrases

Well, the connections aren't immediately obvious. I need to think about this a little.
Well, I have to admit that, at first glance, I can't really see much connection between the pictures and the theme.
However, I suppose you could say that the butterfly emerging from the chrysalis shows the idea of ... and that this might reflect how people would feel after doing the course.
I'm afraid to say I'm stumped by this photograph of the ... . Have you any ideas as to how it relates to the topic?
I wonder if it might be a good idea to talk a bit about the title and theme of the course first?
If we think about what people would get from doing a course like that, that may help.

Long turn and follow-up Interview, Part 3

a Choose one of the prompt cards below. You have ten seconds to think briefly about the topic, then you should talk to the rest of the class for about two minutes. Your teacher will indicate when two minutes have passed, and give you feedback on your performance.

Prompt card a

> To what extent can people change themselves for the better?
> ▶ mental attitudes and thought processes
> ▶ habits and behaviour
> ▶ skills

Prompt card b

> Should cloning be legal?
> ▶ animals
> ▶ humans
> ▶ spare body parts

b Listen carefully to the person who is talking. Your teacher will choose one person to answer a follow-up question on this talk. Your answer should last about a minute.

c Now work with a partner and discuss these questions. You have about one minute to discuss each question.
- *To what extent is self-criticism a useful tool?*
- *If the genetic engineering of humans was legal, which traits would it be unethical to alter?*

Discussion Interview, Part 3

Work with a different partner. Choose one of the following questions to discuss together. Your discussion should last about three minutes. Your teacher will indicate when three minutes have passed. If you have run out of things to say before then, move on to one of the other questions.

> - How important is someone's genetic make-up in the formation of their character?
> - Will the latest discoveries in genetic engineering bring about a change in society's moral values?
> - Is change always a good thing?
> - How influential are our parents' ideas on the way we think and behave as adults?

Media and communication

Listening A

Think about the topic

1 Do the electronic media give us a deeper understanding of the world around us or confuse us with too much irrelevant information?

2 Do you think that modern telecommunications pose a threat to our civil liberties?

Listening 1   Exam task, Part 1

◖◗ You will hear four separate extracts, two from a radio programme about women whose partners like the Internet, and two from a conversation in a pub. For questions **1–8**, choose the answer (**A**, **B** or **C**) which fits best according to what you hear.

Extract 1

You will hear a woman called Shona talking about her boyfriend.

1 When her boyfriend turned up late to dinner, Shona's anger was made worse by the fact that

   A he didn't apologise.

   B he gave her an over-complicated excuse for his lateness.

   C he failed to notice that he was boring her.

                                      `1`

2 Why did Steve take Shona out to a restaurant?

   A To tell her about his new friends.

   B To conciliate her.

   C To try and save their relationship.   `2`

Extract 3

You will hear part of a conversation between three colleagues – Bob, Kevin and Jane.

5 What does Bob think about football nowadays?

   A No one likes going to the stadium anymore.

   B It's more professional than it used to be.   `5`

   C It's more fun than before.

6 What do the men disagree about?

   A The extent to which football has become commercial.

   B Whether TV companies should buy football teams.   `6`

   C The advantages of subscription TV.

Extract 2

You will hear a woman called Mary talking about her husband.

3 What does Mary's husband do when he stays at home?

   A He works until 4 a.m.

   B He forgets to do his work.   `3`

   C He does his work quickly.

4 Mary finds the information her husband gets from the Internet

   A interesting.

   B useful.   `4`

   C trivial.

Extract 4

You will hear a second extract from the conversation between Bob, Kevin and Jane

7 What does Jane think about televised sport?

   A It appeals to young girls.

   B It will become increasingly popular.   `7`

   C It is overrated.

8 How does Bob feel about Kevin's memory for statistics?

   A Scornful.

   B Impressed.   `8`

   C Jealous.

exam tip

In addition to being properly spelt, answers in sentence completion exercises should be correctly punctuated and any abbreviations correctly used. Make sure that you know:
- how to use apostrophes, e.g. *the researcher's findings* (one researcher) compared to *the researchers' findings* (more than one researcher).
- when to use capital letters, e.g. for proper names, names of institutions or organisations, names of religious festivals, etc.
- common abbreviations: a.m., p.m., mins, secs, mph, kg, etc.

Listening 2 | Exam task, Part 2

a 🔲 You will hear a radio broadcast about the potential health risk of using mobile phones. For questions **1–9**, complete the sentences with one or two words, or a short phrase.

The use of mobile phones is on the rise in Britain even though many people have experienced unpleasant **[1]_____** which are associated with their use.

These are believed to be caused by the phones emitting **[2]_____**.

An even more serious potential hazard is that **[3]_____** may be damaged.

The **[4]_____** given to users to protect them from this risk is now thought to have been erroneous, or even dangerous.

A new **[5]_____** which fits into the phone battery may at last provide the answer to this potential health problem.

However, a different study found that health problems may be caused by the handsets giving off **[6]_____** when they heat up.

It is thought that users might inhale these as they talk, or absorb them when the handset comes into contact with their **[7]_____**.

Although the **[8]_____** found no link between mobile phones and health problems, the British authorities are not convinced.

Their **[9]_____** are that adults strictly limit their use of mobiles and that children have recourse to them only in emergencies.

b Now listen again and check, complete or amend your answers.

Speaking A

Commenting on the photographs Interview, Part 2

Work with a partner. Look at photographs **1** and **2**. Compare and contrast the people, activities and atmosphere in each of these photographs. You have about a minute for this.

Collaborative task Interview, Part 2

Work with a partner. Imagine that a media studies student is doing a project on the subject of leisure technology and whether it fosters or destroys our social relationships. She is looking for photographs to illustrate the report she will write. Discuss how each of the photographs relates to the topic of the project and decide what other images it might be appropriate to include. You have about three minutes to talk about this.

> **exam tip**
>
> Remember that you should always talk about **all** the photographs/illustrations that you see before reaching any decision about which to choose or what others to add.

Long turn and follow-up Interview, Part 3

a Choose one of the prompt cards below. You have ten seconds to think briefly about the topic, then you should talk to the rest of the class for about two minutes. Your teacher will indicate when two minutes have passed.

Prompt card a

To what extent is seeing sports live better than watching them on television?

▶ atmosphere

▶ comfort and safety

▶ following what's going on

Prompt card b

What changes have resulted from the advent of the Internet?

▶ shopping habits

▶ use of public services, e.g. libraries, post offices

▶ computer crime

b Listen carefully to the person who is talking. Your teacher will choose one person to answer a follow-up question on this talk. Your answer should last about a minute.

c Now work with a partner and discuss these questions. You have about one minute to discuss each question.

- *Is subscription TV a good idea?*
- *How widespread is Internet use in your country?*

---

exam tip

If you can't recall a word you know during the Interview
- don't remain silent while trying to remember it.
- explain your problem, e.g.
  I can't recall the exact word. or *The word's slipped my mind.*
- try to use a synonym or paraphrase what you want to say, e.g.
  I don't remember the correct term, but it's a device which connects computers to the telephone line.

Discussion Interview, Part 3

Work with a different partner. Choose one of the following questions to discuss together. Your discussion should last about three minutes. Your teacher will indicate when three minutes have passed. If you have run out of things to say before then, move on to one of the other questions.

- Do the benefits of mobile phones outweigh their risks?
- What televised events of the last century do you think made a lasting impression on those who watched them?
- Are there any situations in which radio is a superior medium to television?

Listening B

Listening 1 | Exam task, Part 3

a ▣▢ You will hear a radio programme about invasion of privacy. For questions **1–5**, choose the answer (**A**, **B**, **C** or **D**) which fits best according to what you hear.

1 Caroline Carey

    A has had disagreements with press photographers.
    B considers herself a celebrity.
    C thinks the press will make her more famous.
    D is followed day and night by photographers.

            1

2 At her father's funeral, she

    A agreed to pose for a photographer.
    B swore at a photographer.
    C resented the tabloid press covering the event.
    D felt she had behaved in a disrespectful manner.

            2

3 Laws against invasion of privacy

    A are not acceptable in a democratic country.
    B exist only in America.
    C are rarely obeyed.
    D do not protect public figures.

            3

4 Law courts

    A enforce celebrities' rights of privacy.
    B may acquit photographers who have committed acts of violence.
    C can limit photographers' activities.
    D could restrict the freedom of the press.

            4

5 Jason Wyatt argues that

    A a big story can add ten million copies to a newspaper's circulation.
    B scandal subsidises serious news.
    C readers want more serious news coverage.
    D celebrities enjoy seeing photos of themselves in the press.

            5

b Now listen again and check, complete or amend your answers.

Listening 2 Exam task, Part 4

a ▭ You will hear two people, Ruth and Mike, taking part in a radio debate. They are discussing the effects of TV on children. For questions **1–6** decide whether the opinions are expressed by only one of the speakers, or whether the speakers agree.

Write: (R) for Ruth, (M) for Mike or (B) for both, where they agree.

1 The more violence one sees on screen, the less one is upset by it.

2 Children may be discouraged from violence if they see innocent victims being harmed on screen.

3 The storylines of many films or cartoons are simplistic.

4 TV programmes should illustrate that violence is not an acceptable method of solving problems.

5 Parents should control the number and type of programmes their children watch.

6 Children should be invited to discuss the good and bad points of programmes they've watched.

	1
	2
	3
	4
	5
	6

b Now listen again and check, complete or amend your answers.

---

exam tips

Remember these points during the Listening paper of the exam.

- If you have difficulty with a question, don't spend time worrying about it, as this may prevent you hearing the answers to other questions which come later in the recording. You will always hear each recording twice, so you can concentrate on answering the problem question then.

- At the end of the Listening paper you must transfer all your answers to the special answer sheet. You will be given five minutes to do this. As the answer sheets are marked by computer, make sure you complete the answer sheet in **exactly** the way the instructions tell you to do it.

Speaking B

Personal questions Interview, Part 1

Work with a partner. Each of you should answer one question from each group (**A**, **B** and **C**) below.
You should talk for a total of about three minutes.

A Do you live near your
school or work?

Do you still live with your
parents?

B What kind of house or flat
do you live in?

What do you do in your
spare time?

C Are there any countries you would
particularly like to visit?

Do you think you will continue to use
English in your work or studies?

Commenting on the photographs Interview, Part 2

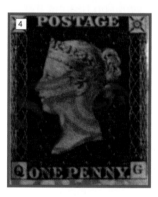

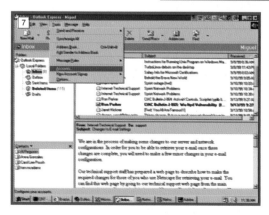

Work with a partner. Look at photograph **1** and talk about who you think would buy a phone
like this, and how useful such devices really are. You have about a minute for this.

Collaborative task Interview, Part 2

Work with a partner. Imagine that the company which produces the phone shown in photograph **1** is about to launch a campaign advertising this product. The theme of the campaign is to be *'Landmarks in Communications Technology'*. The newspaper and magazine advertisements will feature photograph **1** and four of the other images. Talk together about the other images and how they relate to the theme of the campaign, and decide which pictures it would be appropriate to include. You have about three minutes to talk about this.

Long turn and follow-up Interview, Part 3

a Choose one of the prompt cards below. You have ten seconds to think briefly about the topic, then you should talk to the rest of the class for about two minutes. Your teacher will indicate when two minutes have passed.

Prompt card a

> To what extent have newspapers been supplanted by other sources of news?
>
> ▶ local news
> ▶ national news
> ▶ international news

Prompt card b

> To what extent are people influenced by the media?
>
> ▶ opinions
> ▶ lifestyles
> ▶ fashions

b Listen carefully to the person who is talking. Your teacher will choose one person to answer a follow-up question on this talk. Your answer should last about a minute.

c Now work with a partner and discuss these questions. You have about one minute to discuss each question.

- *Are women that often feature in the media appropriate role models?*
- *Should the paparazzi's activities be curtailed?*

Discussion Interview, Part 3

Work with a different partner. Choose one of the following questions to discuss together. Your discussion should last about three minutes. Your teacher will indicate when three minutes have passed. If you have run out of things to say before then, move on to one of the other questions.

- To what extent should parents exercise control over their children's TV viewing habits?
- Is freedom of the press always a good thing?
- Is faster communication necessarily better communication?

exam tips

During your interview:
- do not let the other candidate dominate the discussions – make use of all the opportunities you are given to speak. The only time when it is not appropriate to contribute is during his/her long turn.
- make your responses an appropriate length. This means avoiding long monologues, except when giving your talk during your long turn.

Listening

Part one

You will hear four different extracts. For questions **1–8**, choose the answer (**A**, **B** or **C**) which fits best according to what you hear. There are two questions for each extract.

Extract One

You will hear a couple discussing getting a dog.

1 What is the main reason the man wants a dog?

   A To protect his property.

   B To reassure his wife.

   C To keep his family company when he is away.

           `1`

2 What do the man and his wife disagree about?

   A The type of dog they should buy.

   B The possibility of a dog attacking their child.

   C The effectiveness of a dog in deterring intruders.

           `2`

Extract Two

You will hear part of a talk given by a guide as she shows visitors round a stately home.

3 The subject of the portrait may have gone abroad

   A because his favourite brother died.

   B as a result of a scandal.

   C in order to join the Indian army.

           `3`

4 The duke married his wife

   A for her looks.

   B for money.

   C for love.

           `4`

Extract Three

You will hear two friends, one of whom has returned to Britain after several years abroad, having a conversation.

5 What do they disagree about?

    A The extent to which British shops have improved.

    B The extent to which town centres have altered.

    C The extent to which consumerism has taken over in Britain.

        5

6 What is the woman's opinion of Britain nowadays?

    A It is more cosmopolitan but less interesting than before.

    B It is more sophisticated but less efficient than before.

    C It is more diverse and more pleasant than before.

        6

Extract Four

You will hear the review of a new film on the radio.

7 The director usually makes

    A thrillers.

    B love stories.

    C biographical films.

 7

8 The leading actress is praised for

    A her beauty and sensitivity.

    B taking on a role that other actresses turned down.

    C handling a difficult role well.

        8

Part two

You will hear a radio report about new developments in computing. For questions **9–17**, complete the sentences with a word or short phrase.

Computers are now much smaller and more powerful than they used to be thanks to developments in **9** [ ] .

Further miniaturisation could be achieved if computers could be controlled by the user's **10** [ ] processes.

Research into this possibility is now being carried out on **11** [ ] .

Glass implants containing **12** [ ] are placed in the part of the brain which controls movement.

Once nerves have grown inside the implants, signals can be sent to a computer by means of **13** [ ] .

Using this system, one participant in the research has learnt to move **14** [ ] by imagining himself moving parts of his body.

Communication by this means is currently somewhat **15** [ ] but is still exceedingly helpful to people who cannot communicate in any other way.

There are fears that this may be the first step towards computers being used to **16** [ ] .

However, experts think the **17** [ ] of the technology outweigh objections of an ethical nature.

Part three

You will hear an interview with Faye Davison, who set up a website which reunites old school friends. For questions **18–22**, choose the answer (**A**, **B**, **C** or **D**) which fits best according to what you hear.

18 Many Internet enterprises fail because

    A their business idea is not original enough.

    B it's not easy to generate income through online businesses.   18

    C they fail to attract enough visitors to their site.

    D they can't stay in business long enough to become profitable.

19 At the time she set the site up, Faye

    A had just accepted a new job.

    B was working for an insurance company.   19

    C was working on freelance computer projects.

    D was temporarily unemployed.

20 When Faye decided to get in touch with some old school friends

    A it was difficult to find where they now lived.

    B she found most of them had got married.   20

    C not many of them wanted to meet up again.

    D she wished she could have used an Internet site to contact them.

21 OldPals.com earns money by

    A running advertisements on the site.

    B charging members a monthly fee.   21

    C charging people when they first use the site's facilities.

    D charging a fee to visit the site.

22 Faye thinks people are motivated to get in touch with old classmates mainly

    A at times of crisis in their lives.

    B because they were happier when they were younger.   22

    C by curiosity.

    D because they want to see who's made a better success of their lives.

Part four

You will hear two colleagues, Linda and John, discussing men and women's roles at work and in society. For questions **23–28**, decide whether the opinions are expressed by only one of the speakers, or whether the speakers agree.

Write: (L) for Linda, (J) for John or (B) for both, where they agree.

23	Men and women relate to their friends differently.	23
24	Women are under more pressure than men.	24
25	The media foster unreal expectations in women.	25
26	Women are paid less than men.	26
27	Unemployment undermines men's self-respect.	27
28	Neither men nor women respect men who bring up children.	28

Speaking

Part 1 (3 minutes)

Each candidate: Answer one question from each of these groups.

- Do you live near here?
- Do you live alone or with your family?

- Could you tell us something about your current job or studies?
- What have you enjoyed most about learning English?

- Would you like to live and work in an English-speaking country?
- What are your plans for the future?

Part 2 (4 minutes)

Both candidates: Look at photograph **4** on page 90 and discuss what you think happened just before it was taken and how the people shown in the photograph may be feeling. You have about one minute for this.

Both candidates: Now look at all the photographs on page 90. Imagine that a photographic gallery in your town is mounting an exhibition on the theme of 'Progress'. Discuss together what aspects of the theme each of these pictures illustrates. Then suggest three other images representing 'Progress' which you think should be included in the exhibition. You have about three minutes for this.

Part 3 (12 minutes)

Candidate A: Look at prompt card **a** below and say what you think about the question written on it. There are also some ideas on the card for you to use if you like. You have two minutes to talk about the question.

Prompt card a

> To what extent is making progress in your chosen career the result of talent?
>
> ▶ training
>
> ▶ luck
>
> ▶ contacts

Candidate B: What do you think?

Both candidates: Discuss **one** of the questions below.

- Do you think talent is something you are born with?
- Should people who have gained a university degree earn more than those who have not?

Candidate B: Look at prompt card **b** below and say what you think about the question written on it. There are also some ideas on the card for you to use if you like. You have two minutes to talk about the question.

Prompt card b

> What problems have been created by scientific and technological progress?
>
> ▶ the environment
>
> ▶ employment
>
> ▶ food production

Candidate A: Is there anything you would like to add?

Both candidates: Discuss **one** of the questions below.

- Do you think increasing automation means that in future people won't need to work?
- To what extent do people eat more healthily now than they used to do?

Both candidates: Now discuss some of these questions about progress in general.

- What medical breakthrough would you most like to see in the near future?
- Is a higher standard of living more desirable than quality of life?
- Does the advent of cloning and 'designer babies' represent progress for the human race?
- What is the greatest threat to progress in the world today?

Mini-dictionary

Unit 1

affluent (adj) having plenty of money, so that you can afford to buy expensive things, live in a nice house, etc.

assessment (n) a process in which you make a judgment about a person or situation

contemplative (adj) spending a lot of time thinking seriously and quietly

convey (v) to communicate information or a message

correspondence (n) letters exchanged between people, especially official or business letters

cramped (adj) a cramped room, building, etc. does not have enough space for the people in it

eliminate (v) to completely get rid of something that is unnecessary or unwanted

encompass (v) to include a wide range of ideas, subjects, etc.

nerve-wracking (adj) nerve-wracking situation makes you feel very nervous because it is difficult or frightening

nevertheless (adv) in spite of a fact that you have just mentioned

open-plan (adj) an open-plan office, school, etc. does not have walls dividing it into separate rooms

sedentary (adj) a sedentary job is done while sitting down, and without moving around very much

solitary (adj) spending a lot of time alone, usually because you like being alone

somewhat (adv) more than a little but not very

state-of-the art (adj) using the most modern and recently-developed methods, materials or knowledge

terribly (adv) extremely

workstation (n) the part of an office where you work, where your desk, computer, etc. are

Unit 2

arson (n) the crime of deliberately making something burn, especially a building

bleach (n) a chemical used to make things white or to kill germs

bumper (n) a bar fixed on the front or back of a car to protect the car when it knocks against anything; **bumper-to-bumper** (phr) (for cars) very close together and moving slowly

car-pooling (n phr) a system whereby several people share one car to go to work, in order to save petrol and protect the environment

chunk (n) a large piece of something that does not have an even shape

compensation (n) money that someone pays you because they have harmed or hurt you in some way

traffic congestion (n phr) a large number of vehicles on a road or in a town that cannot move, or that can only move very slowly

conjure up (phr v) to bring a thought, picture, idea or memory to someone's mind

detergent (n) a liquid or powder that contains soap used for washing clothes, dishes, etc.

disregard (n) to ignore something or treat it as unimportant

disruption (n) a situation in which something is prevented from continuing in its normal way because of problems and difficulties

dump (n) a place where unwanted waste is taken and left

elicit (v) to succeed in getting information or a reaction from someone, especially when this is difficult

go up in flames (v phr) to explode or be destroyed by fire

heap (n) a large untidy pile of things

infrastructure (n) the basic systems and structures that a country or organisation needs in order to work properly, for example transport, communications and banking systems

legislation (n) a law or set of laws

on stand-by (prep phr) ready to help immediately if you are needed

provision (n) the act of providing something that someone needs

rubble (n) (a mass of) broken stones or bricks, esp. from a building that has been destroyed

shatter (v) to break suddenly into very small pieces, or to make something break in this way

stimulating (adj) exciting or full of new ideas

tremor (n) a small earthquake in which the ground shakes slightly

widespread (adj) existing or happening in many places or situations, or among many people

Unit 3

have the odds stacked against you (phr) to be at a great disadvantage

beast of burden (n phr) an animal, such as a horse or donkey, which carries things

bond (with) (v) to develop a special relationship with someone

burden (n) something that is carried; load

cape (n) a long loose piece of clothing without sleeves that fastens around your neck and hangs from your shoulders

cheetah (n) a member of the cat family that has long legs and black spots on its fur, and can run extremely fast

convivial (adj) pleasantly merry and friendly

domestic (adj) used in the house or home

dispute (n) a situation in which two countries or groups of people quarrel or disagree with each other

distasteful (adj) very unpleasant or morally offensive

distressed (adj) extremely upset and shocked

factory farming (n phr) the practice or business of farms where animals are kept in small cages and made to grow or produce eggs, milk, etc. very quickly

gathering (n) a meeting of a group of people

goad (v) to make someone do something by annoying them or encouraging them until they do it

harassed (adj) anxious and tired because you have too many problems or things to do

hide (n) an animal's skin, especially when it has been removed to be used for leather

highchair (n) a special tall chair that a young child sits in to eat

humiliate (v) to make someone feel ashamed and upset, especially by making them seem stupid or weak

ill-treatment (n phr) cruelty to someone, especially to a child or animal

intimate (adj) having an extremely close relationship

laundry (n) clothes, sheets, etc. that need to be washed or have just been washed

odds (n) how likely it is that something will or will not happen, especially when this can be stated in numbers

on the whole (phr) used to say that something is generally true

outweigh (v) to be more important or valuable than something else

overwrought (adj) very upset, nervous and worried

primarily (adv) mainly

propose a toast (v phr) to formally ask a group of people at a social event to join you in wishing someone success and happiness while raising a glass of wine and then drinking it

qualify (v) to have the right to claim something

rear (v) to look after a person or animal until they are fully grown

repellent (adj) nasty or very unpleasant

urban (adj) connected with a town or city

withdraw (v) to no longer take part in or belong to an organisation

wrangle (v) to argue with someone angrily for a long time

Unit 4

alleviate (v) to make something less painful or difficult

ballot (n) 1 a system of secret voting or an occasion when you vote in this way; 2 a piece of paper on which you make a secret vote

beggar (n) someone who lives by asking people for food and money

booth (n) a small partly enclosed place where one person can do something privately, such as use the telephone or vote

civil war (n phr) a war in which opposing groups of people from the same country fight each other in order to gain political control

collaborative (adj) involving two or more people working together to achieve something

curriculum (n) the subjects that are taught by a school, college, etc., or the things that are studied in a particular subject

guerrilla (n) a member of an unofficial military group, especially one fighting to remove a government from power, that attacks its enemies in small groups unexpectedly

innovative (adj) using clever new ideas and methods

lax (adj) not strict or careful enough about standards of behaviour, work, safety, etc.

minor (n) a person below the age (usually 18, as in Britain, the USA, Greece) at which they are fully responsible in law for their actions

participative (adj) involving everyone

recruit (v) to get people to join the army or navy

rote learning (n phr) a method of learning that involves repeating something until you remember it, without having to understand it

warrior (n) a soldier or man experienced in fighting, especially in the past

Unit 5

apathetic (adj) not excited about something and not caring whether it happens, or not interested in anything and unwilling to make an effort to change and improve things

be bound to (v phr) to be very likely to do or feel a particular thing

chubby (adj) fat in a pleasant healthy-looking way

degenerative (adj) a degenerative illness gradually gets worse and cannot be stopped

enhance (v) to improve something

evaluate (v) to carefully consider something to see how useful or valuable it is

glow (v) the bright colour your face or body has after exercise or when you are very pleased and excited

hereditary (adj) mental or physical qualities, abilities or illnesses, etc. that are hereditary are passed from parent to child in the cells of the body

immune system (n phr) the system by which your body protects itself against disease

infant mortality (n phr) deaths of babies

infectious (adj) an infectious illness can be passed from one person to another, especially through the air you breathe

jeopardise (v) to risk losing or spoiling something important or valuable

lease of life (n phr) if something has a new lease of life, improvements are made that mean it will last longer

longevity (n) long life

monitor (n) to carefully watch and check a situation in order to see how it changes or progresses over a period of time

nose job (n phr) a medical operation on one's nose to change one's appearance

nutrient (n) a chemical or food that provides what is needed for life and growth

predisposition (n) a tendency to behave in a particular way or suffer from a particular illness

prolong (v) to deliberately make something such as a feeling or activity last longer

respiratory (adj) connected with breathing

surrogate mother (n phr) a woman who has a baby for another woman who cannot have one

vaccination (n) a process by which someone is protected from a disease by having a small amount of a substance containing that disease put into their body

vigorous (adj) using a lot of energy and strength or determination

Unit 6

apparent (adj) easily noticed or understood

barely (adv) in a way that almost does not happen, exist, etc.

by and large (prep phr) used when talking generally about someone or something

combat (v) to take action in an organised way in order to oppose something bad or harmful

consumer durables (n pl) large things such as cars, televisions and furniture, that you do not buy often

contempt (n) a feeling that someone or something is not important and deserves no respect

devise (v) to plan or invent a way of doing something, especially something complicated and clever

gimmick (n) a trick or an object that makes you notice a product and want to buy it

greed (n) a strong desire for more food or drink than you need

excessive (adj) much more than is reasonable or necessary

mirror (v) if something mirrors a situation, fact, belief, etc., it is very similar to it and gives a clear idea of what it is like

prime time (n phr) the time in the evening when the greatest number of people are watching television

resemblance (n) a similarity between two things, especially in the way they look

restrict (v) to limit or control the size, amount or range of something

vulnerable (adj) someone who is vulnerable is easily harmed or hurt emotionally, physically or morally

Unit 7

attribute (v) to say that a situation or event is caused by something

balaclava (n) a warm woollen hat that covers most of your head and face

bear in mind (v phr) to remember a fact or piece of information that is important or could be useful in the future

demographic (adj) connected with the study of human populations and the ways in which they change

firearm (n) a small gun that can be carried

grab (v) to take hold of someone or something with a sudden or violent movement

hold up (phr v) to rob or try to rob a place by using violence

justice (n) 1 fairness in the way people are treated; 2 the system by which people are judged in courts of law and criminals are punished

juvenile (adj) connected with young people who are not yet adults

on patrol (prep phr) if a police officer is on patrol, he/she goes around different parts of an area at regular times to check that there is no trouble or danger

pang (n) a sudden feeling of pain, sadness, etc.

peer pressure (n phr) a strong feeling that you must do the same things as other people of your age if you want them to like you

penalty (n) a punishment for breaking a law, rule or legal agreement

beyond redemption (phr) too bad to be saved, repaired or improved

rehabilitation (n) the process by which someone is helped to live a healthy, useful or active life again after they have been seriously ill or in prison

reoffend (v) to commit a crime for a second, third, etc. time

retribution (n) severe punishment that is deserved

snatch (v) to take something away from someone with a quick violent movement

tricks of the trade (n pl) clever methods used in a particular job

Unit 8

amateur (adj) not doing something as your job, but only for pleasure or interest

auction (n) a public meeting where land, buildings, paintings, etc. are sold to the person who offers the most money for them

auctioneer (n) someone who is in charge of an auction and tells people the prices of the goods

awe (n) a feeling of great respect and admiration for someone or something

backgammon (n) a game for two players, using flat round pieces and dice on a special board

bagpipes (n pl) a musical instrument played especially in Scotland in which air stored in a bag is forced out through pipes to produce the sound

bid (v) to offer to pay a particular price for goods, especially in an auction

budget (n) a plan of how a person or organisation will spend the money that is available in a particular period of time, or the money itself

clay (n) heavy sticky soil that can be used for making pots, bricks, etc.

currency (n) the system or type of money that a particular country uses

diminish (v) to become or make something become smaller or less important

easel (n) a wooden frame that you put a painting on while you paint it

embody (v) if a person, thing or organisation embodies an idea or principle it clearly expresses it and shows its importance by the way it behaves or affects behaviour

festive (adj) (of atmosphere, season, etc.) suitable for a special occasion or special event, marked by public enjoyment

go under the hammer (v phr) to be offered for sale at an auction

Gothic (adj) the Gothic style of building was common in Western Europe between the 12th and 16th centuries. Its main features were pointed arches tall pillars and tall thin pointed windows

heritage (n) important qualities, customs and traditions that have been in a society for a long time

hushed (adj) quiet because people are listening, waiting to hear something or talking quietly

illuminate (v) to make a light shine on something, or fill a place with light

kiln (n) a special oven for baking clay pots, bricks, etc.

kilt (v) a type of thick skirt, traditionally worn by Scottish men

mandatory (adj) something that is mandatory must be done because the law says it must be done; compulsory, obligatory

reverential (adj) showing respect

scrutinise (v) to examine very closely and carefully

spire (n) a roof that rises steeply to a point on top of a tower, especially on a church

still life (n phr) a picture of an arrangement of objects, especially flowers and fruit

subdued (adj) subdued lighting, colours, etc. are less bright than usual

subsidise (v) to pay part of the cost of something so that the buyer can pay less for it

vocational (adj) vocational training/guidance, etc. – training, etc. that teaches you the skills you need to do a particular job

watercolour (n) paint that you mix with water and use for painting pictures

Unit 9

adapt (v) to gradually change your behaviour and attitudes so that you get used to a new situation and can deal with it successfully

be stumped (v phr) when someone asks such a difficult question that you are completely unable to think of an answer

bulge (v) to stick out in a rounded shape, especially because something is very full or too tight

chrysalis (n) a moth or butterfly at the stage of development when it has a hard outer shell, before being a larva and an adult

coals (n pl) a piece of coal (a black mineral which is dug from the earth and burnt to produce heat), especially one that is burning

drench (v) to make something or someone extremely wet

emerge (v) to appear or come out from somewhere

gleam (v) to shine softly

oblivious (adj) not knowing about, or not noticing, something that is happening around you

on the verge of (prep phr) about to do something

sculptured (adj) to describe something that has a clear shape as if it had been made by an artist

strain (v) to damage or weaken (oneself or a part of the body) through too much effort or pressure

torso (n) your body, not including your head, arms or legs

tranquil (adj) pleasantly calm, quiet and peaceful

triumphant (adj) expressing pleasure and pride because of your victory or success

unleash (v) to suddenly let a strong force, feeling, etc. have its full effect

urge (n) a strong wish or need

Unit 10

curtail (v) to reduce something such as the amount of money you spend

foster (v) to help a skill, feeling, idea, etc. develop over a period of time

lasting (adj) strong enough, well enough planned, etc. to last for a very long time

paparazzi (n pl) newspaper writers or photographers who follow famous people

subscription (n) an amount of money you pay regularly to be a member of an organisation or to help its work

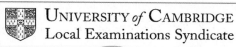

UNIVERSITY *of* CAMBRIDGE
Local Examinations Syndicate

SAMPLE

Candidate Name
If not already printed, write name
in CAPITALS and complete the
Candidate No. grid (in pencil).

Candidate Signature

Examination Title

Centre

Supervisor:

If the candidate is ABSENT or has WITHDRAWN shade here ⬜

Centre No.

Candidate No.

Examination Details

0	0	0	0
1	1	1	1
2	2	2	2
3	3	3	3
4	4	4	4
5	5	5	5
6	6	6	6
7	7	7	7
8	8	8	8
9	9	9	9

Candidate Answer Sheet CPE Paper 4 Listening

Mark test version (in PENCIL)	A ⬜	B ⬜	C ⬜	Special arrangements	S ⬜	H ⬜

Instructions
Use a PENCIL (B or HB).
Rub out any answer you wish to change using an eraser.

For **Parts 1 and 3**:
Mark ONE letter only for each question.
For example, if you think B is the right answer,
mark your answer sheet like this:

0	A ⬜	B	C ⬜

For **Part 2**:
Write your answer clearly in
the space like this:

0	example

For **Part 4**:
Write ONE letter only, like this:

0	A

Part 1

1	A ⬜	B ⬜	C ⬜
2	A ⬜	B ⬜	C ⬜
3	A ⬜	B ⬜	C ⬜
4	A ⬜	B ⬜	C ⬜
5	A ⬜	B ⬜	C ⬜
6	A ⬜	B ⬜	C ⬜
7	A ⬜	B ⬜	C ⬜
8	A ⬜	B ⬜	C ⬜

Part 2

		Do not write here
9		1 9 0
10		1 10 0
11		1 11 0
12		1 12 0
13		1 13 0
14		1 14 0
15		1 15 0
16		1 16 0
17		1 17 0

Part 3

18	A ⬜	B ⬜	C ⬜	D ⬜
19	A ⬜	B ⬜	C ⬜	D ⬜
20	A ⬜	B ⬜	C ⬜	D ⬜
21	A ⬜	B ⬜	C ⬜	D ⬜
22	A ⬜	B ⬜	C ⬜	D ⬜

Part 4

		Do not write here
23		1 23 0
24		1 24 0
25		1 25 0
26		1 26 0
27		1 27 0
28		1 28 0

CPE 4

DP440/349